## Collins

**Student Support Materials for Edexcel A2 History**

# Unit 3 E2

A world divided: Superpower relations, 1944–90

Series editor: Angela Leonard

Authors: Andrew Mitchell, Robin Bunce and Laura Gallagher

William Collins' dream of knowledge for all began with the publication of his first book in 1819. A self-educated mill worker, he not only enriched millions of lives, but also founded a flourishing publishing house. Today, staying true to this spirit, Collins books are packed with inspiration, innovation and practical expertise. They place you at the centre of a world of possibility and give you exactly what you need to explore it.

Collins. Freedom to teach

Published by Collins
An imprint of HarperCollins Publishers
77–85 Fulham Palace Road
Hammersmith
London
W6 8JB

Browse the complete Collins catalogue at
www.collinseducation.com

© HarperCollins Publishers Limited 2012

10 9 8 7 6 5

ISBN 978 0 00 745744 1

Andrew Mitchell, Laura Gallagher and Robin Bunce assert their moral rights to be identified as the authors of this work

British Library Cataloguing in Publication Data
A Catalogue record for this publication is available from the British Library

Commissioned by Andrew Campbell
Project managed by Alexandra Riley and Shirley Wakley
Production by Simon Moore

Designed by Jouve
Edited by Gudrun Kaiser
Proofread by Maggie Rumble and Grace Glendinning
Indexed by Michael Forder
Illustrations by Ann Paganuzzi
Picture and text research by Grace Glendinning and Caroline Green
Cover photo research by Caroline Green
Cover design by Angela English
Technical review by Geoffrey Stewart

Cover Acknowledgement: Mushroom Cloud During Atomic Weapons Test, by Roger Ressmeyer, supplied by Corbis.

**Acknowledgements**
The publishers gratefully acknowledge the permission granted to reproduce the copyright material in this book. While every effort has been made to trace and contact copyright holders, where this has not been possible the publishers will be pleased to make the necessary arrangements at the first opportunity.

p 7 From Fraser J. Harbutt, *Yalta 1945: Europe and America at the Crossroads*, 2010. Used with permission from Cambridge University Press; p 9 From John Young and John Kent, *International Relations Since 1945*, 2004. By permission of Oxford University Press; p 13t Reprinted by permission of the publisher from AMERICA'S COLD WAR: THE POLITICS OF INSECURITY by Campbell Craig and Fredik Logevall, p. 131, Cambridge, Mass.: The Belknap Press of Harvard University Press, Copyright (c) 2009 by the President and Fellow of Harvard College; p 13b From Jussi M. Hanhimäki and Odd

Arne Westad, *The Cold War*, 2004. By permission of Oxford University Press; pp 14, 16 & 81 From Robert J. McMahon, *The Cold War: A Very Short Introduction*, 2003. By permission of Oxford University Press; p 20 From Walter LaFeber, *America, Russia and the Cold War 1945–1992*, 7th edition, 1993. Published by Mcgraw-Hill; p 21 From Louis J. Halle, *The Cold War as History*, 1971. Published by Harper & Row; p 24t From John Lewis Gaddis, *We Now Know*, 1997. By Permission of Clarendon Press, an imprint of Oxford University Press; p 24bl From Richard Crockatt, The United States and the Cold War 1941–53, 1989. Published by the British Association for American Studies; p 24br From Robert Dallek, *Franklin D. Roosevelt and American Foreign Policy, 1932–45*, 1979. By permission of Oxford University Press; pp 26 & 84 From *The Cold War*, Jeremy Isaacs and Taylor Downing, published by Little, Brown Book Group in 2008. Reprinted with permission from Little, Brown Book Group and Peters, Fraser & Dunlop; p 77 From *Reagan, Bush, Gorbachev: revisiting the end of the Cold War*, Norman A. Graebner, Richard Dean Burns, Joseph M. Siracusa © 2008 by Praeger Security International, 88 Post Road West, Westport, CT 06881, an imprint of Greenwood Publishing Group, Inc. Reproduced with permission of ABC-CLIO, Santa Barbara, CA; p 86 From *The Cold War: An International History*, p.115, David S. Painter, Routledge, 1999; p 90 From Joseph Smith, *The Cold War 1945–1991*, 2nd edition. Published by Wiley Blackwell 1998; p 92 From John Lewis Gaddis, `On Starting All Over Again: A Naïve Approach to the Study of the Cold War' in Odd Arne Westad (ed.) *Reviewing the Cold War: Approaches, Interpretations, Theory*. Published by Frank Cass 2000; pp 105 & 134t From Eric Hobsbawm, Age of Extremes: *The Short Twentieth Century 1914–1991*, 1994. Published by Michael Joseph and printed with permission of Penguin and David Higham Associates; pp 106t & 134c From John Lewis Gaddis, *The Cold War*, 2006. Published by Penguin and printed with permission; pp 106b & 134b From Michael Burleigh, *Sacred Causes: Religion and Politics from the European Dictators to Al Qaeda*. Reprinted by permission of HarperCollins Publishers Ltd © 2006 Michael Burleigh; p 126t From an article by Arthur M. Schlesinger Jr, `Origins of the Cold War'. Reprinted by permission of FOREIGN AFFAIRS, Journal of Foreign Affairs 46, October 1967 © 1967 by the Council on Foreign Relations, Inc. www.ForeignAffairs.com; p 126c From Vojtech Mastny, *The Cold War and Soviet Insecurity*, 1996. By permission of Oxford University Press; p 126b From Martin McCauley, *Origins of the Cold War 1941–49*, 2008. Published by Longman: Pearson Education.

The publisher would like to thank the following for permission to reproduce pictures in these pages (t = top, b = bottom, c = centre, l = left, r = right):

COVER Roger Ressmeyer/CORBIS, p 9 Bokhach/Shutterstock, p 22, 25, 50b & 73b United States Library of Congress/WikiMedia Commons, p 31 Keystone Pictures USA/Alamy, p 32 Time & Life Pictures/Getty Images, p 50t National Archives and Records Administration/WikiMedia Comons, p 50c Keystone Pictures USA/Alamy, p 54 INTERFOTO/Alamy, p 70 White House Photograph/Courtesy Gerald R. Ford Library/Photographer: David Hume Kennerly/WikiMedia Commons, p 73t Kirsty Pargeter/Shutterstock, p 73c PaulPaladin/Shutterstock, p 73c millerium arkay/Shutterstock, p 76 Courtesy Ronald Reagan Library/WikiMedia Commons.

# Contents

## The origins of the Cold War, 1917–44

### Background to the superpower conflict

The Cold War emerged after the end of the Second World War. The causes of the Cold War go back to the origins of communism during the mid-19th century, the formation of the USSR in the years after the Russian Revolution of 1917, and the legacy of US and Russian involvement during the Second World War.

### Capitalism and communism

From October 1917, when Russia was led by the Communist Party, Russian leaders were attempting to realise the vision set out by Karl Marx, the founder of communism. In 1848, Marx published *The Manifesto of the Communist Party*. Marx argued that human society progressed through a series of stages to capitalism, and then to communism. He believed that under capitalism, the bourgeoisie exploited the proletariat. He argued that this exploitation would lead to a revolution in which the proletariat would overthrow the bourgeoisie and capitalism, and replace it with communism.

In the USA, by contrast, the government believed in the virtues of capitalism. The 'American Dream' was rooted in the capitalist notion that, through hard work, anyone could become rich and powerful.

### Essential notes

Karl Marx was a German philosopher and journalist. Together with his friend, Friedrich Engels, he was the most influential political radical of the 19th century.

Marx argued that capitalist society was dominated by two classes. The bourgeoisie, or middle class, owned the majority of the property; the proletariat, or working class, worked in the factories owned by the bourgeoisie.

### Essential notes

The practice of communism was often quite different from the theory. The table on page 5 outlines how communism worked in the USSR.

|  | Communism | Capitalism |
|---|---|---|
| Focus | Economic equality: redistribution of wealth to ensure that no one is rich and no one is poor.<br><br>Economic rights: the right to work; the right to a decent standard of living. | Political rights: the right to free speech, the right to vote; equality before the law.<br><br>Economic freedom: free trade; *laissez-faire*. |
| Key value | Equality: liberty is meaningless without equality because in reality, poor people are not free. | Individual freedom: the basis of a good society is freedom in the sense that individuals are not subject to oppressive government interference. |
| Style of government | Workers' democracy: society is governed by small, democratic councils that are made up of workers. | Parliamentary democracy: the ability to change the government in free elections; parliaments are elected by the people at regular intervals to make important decisions on their behalf. |
| Criticism of other systems | Capitalism exploits workers: the bourgeoisie make a profit by paying their workers as little as possible. | Communism is unrealistic: inequalities in wealth are natural and inevitable; the government cannot be changed by the people. |

Communism and capitalism in theory

## US–USSR relations, 1917–41

The Russian Revolution of 1917 brought Vladimir Lenin into power. Publically committed to creating the first communist society, he was a fierce critic of capitalism and encouraged revolution in all economically developed nations. However, Lenin's call to replace capitalism with communism worried US leaders, and events during 1919 and 1920 formed the basis of the First Red Scare. The US government feared that radicals were plotting its violent overthrow.

The US government refused to recognise Lenin's communist government and there was no trade between the USA and Russia between 1918 and 1924. Trade resumed in 1924 but suspicion continued on both sides.

**Essential notes**

Vladimir Lenin was the leader of the Russian Communist Party. He ruled Russia from 1917 until his death in 1924.

## The Grand Alliance, 1941–5

The Second World War led to a 'marriage of convenience' between the USA and the USSR. Faced with a common enemy – Nazi Germany – the two powers and Great Britain formed the Grand Alliance. During this period, all propaganda criticising one another's new allies was removed. Through the lend-lease scheme, set up in order to help defeat Hitler, the USA provided food and military equipment to the USSR.

Even so, tensions existed at the heart of the relationship. As the war progressed, and after the Nazi defeat, US President Roosevelt and Soviet leader Stalin had very different views about how Europe should be governed. Roosevelt favoured capitalist free trade and parliamentary democracy, while Stalin wanted to remake Eastern Europe in the image of the USSR. The Tehran Conference of 1943 recognised the differences between the capitalist West and the communist East. As a result, it was agreed at the conference to divide post-war Europe into a capitalist sphere of influence in the West and a communist sphere of influence in the East.

The table shows that by 1945, capitalism and communism were very different.

**Essential notes**

The Tehran Conference of 1943 was the first of three meetings between the leaders of the Grand Alliance. 'The Big Three' (Roosevelt, Churchill and Stalin) met to discuss the future of Europe.

|  | 1945: Capitalism in the USA | 1945: Communism in the USSR |
|---|---|---|
| Economy | *Laissez-faire* economy: government plays a minor role in the economy; the production and distribution of goods is organised through a free market. | Government-planned economy: government sets production targets, wages and the price of goods. |
| Government | Representative democracy: two big parties compete for election to Congress and the Presidency; individuals have rights that are protected by the US Constitution. | One-party state: the Communist Party represents the interests of the working class; other parties are not permitted; individual rights are less important than the common good. |

Capitalism in the USA and communism in the USSR: two very different political systems

## The end of the Grand Alliance

In part, the Cold War emerged from disagreements within the Grand Alliance during the years that followed the Second World War. During this period, the great powers had a series of conferences, which were focused more and more on international relations. Initially, the leaders of Russia and the USA were able to collaborate at conferences in Yalta and Potsdam. However, the relationships at the heart of the Grand Alliance were increasingly strained towards the end of 1945.

# The early stages of the Cold War, 1945–9

### The Yalta Conference, 1945

The Yalta Conference was designed to allow senior figures in the Grand Alliance to co-ordinate military strategy as the Second World War drew to a close. In addition, the Big Three (Stalin, Roosevelt and Churchill) published the *Declaration on Liberated Europe*, which outlined their plans for post-war Europe. The Declaration contained the following agreements:

- The three powers agreed to set up interim governments in the territories that they liberated.

- These governments would be representative governments, formed on behalf of 'all democratic elements' within the liberated country.

- The USSR should have a 'sphere of influence' in Eastern Europe.

- The United Nations was to be established in order to ensure world peace.

The Declaration was significant because it suggested unity between the members of the Grand Alliance. However, important differences were glossed over.

One specific difference was the commitment to set up governments that represented 'all democratic elements'. This was interpreted very differently in the East and the West. For Roosevelt and Churchill this represented a commitment to set up parliamentary democracy similar to that of Britain or the USA. For Stalin, a government that represented 'all democratic elements' suggested a government that worked on behalf of workers and peasants, and therefore a government in which the Communist Party played a leading role.

Overall, there were a series of issues that the Yalta Conference was unable to resolve. Examples are: the exact borders of Germany and Poland and the extent to which the defeated powers should pay reparations.

### The Potsdam Conference, 1945

Between the conferences of Yalta and Potsdam, the USSR established governments in the territories it had liberated in Eastern Europe. Britain and the USA refused to recognise these governments because they were unelected. The Western powers were also concerned because the USSR was taking reparations directly from liberated countries. In practice, Stalin ordered factories to be dismantled across Eastern Europe. These were reassembled in Russia, to help to rebuild the Soviet economy after the war. This worried Britain and the USA because they feared it would stifle economic recovery in Eastern Europe, and so leave Eastern European countries economically dependent on the USSR.

Against this background, negotiations at Potsdam were difficult. Indeed, there were problems in reconciling Britain and the USA's commitment to democracy with the USSR's demand for a 'sphere of influence'. Even so, the conference did agree that after the war, Germany would be de-Nazified and disarmed.

Potsdam was significant because, in spite of growing tensions, it demonstrated that the three big powers were still willing to work together.

---

## Essential notes

The United Nations is an international organisation that was established in 1945. Its aim is to promote world peace through international dialogue.

## Essential notes

The term 'sphere of influence' refers to a geographical region over which one country has a significant degree of political, economic and military control.

## Essential notes

Relationships between the major powers in 1945 were strained, partly by traditional great power rivalry. Stalin was keen to regain the territory that had once belonged to the Russian empire, whereas Britain was keen to defend its imperial territories.

## Essential notes

Following Japan's defeat at the end of the Second World War, its territories were divided between the victorious powers. These divisions created further tensions between the USA and the USSR.

## International diplomacy in late 1945

In late 1945, the three major powers met on two occasions. The Council of Foreign Ministers, which met in London in September and October 1945, was the first major failure of diplomacy within the Grand Alliance. The USA and the USSR were unable to resolve their differences over the occupation of Japan, so the Council achieved little. The Moscow Council of December 1945 was more successful, agreeing that each major power should have a 'sphere of influence', as follows:

- USSR – Eastern Europe
- USA – South America Pacific, parts of East and South-East Asia
- Britain – Mediterranean, Middle East.

## Superpower relations by late 1945

Tensions between the USA and the USSR grew, for two major reasons:

- At the end of the 19th century, Britain and Russia had two of the biggest empires in the world. There had been conflict over the Mediterranean and Afghanistan. By 1945, Britain feared losing world influence to the USSR and so attempted to create an Anglo–US Pact. This pulled together the capitalist powers, in opposition to communist Russia.

- Harry Truman, who became President of the USA on Roosevelt's death in April 1945, was under great pressure to stand up to Stalin. The US Congress was outraged that there had been no democratic elections in Eastern Europe, and some congressmen accused Truman of 'appeasing Stalin'.

Tensions were heightened by the vagueness of earlier agreements. Issues such as the relationship between the occupying powers in Germany and Japan created conflict.

Despite all the issues, a working relationship between the superpowers still existed. The Western powers had to accept that they could not force the USSR to establish democratic regimes in Eastern Europe. Equally, they had to accept that it was not in their interests to go to war with the USSR. The Moscow Council created the shared understanding that each great power should have a sphere of influence. This council was significant because it was the last occasion on which the Grand Alliance worked effectively.

### Source 1
(From Fraser J. Harbutt, *Yalta 1945: Europe and America at the Crossroads*, published by Cambridge University Press 2010)

Until the beginning of 1945, it was almost universally assumed that the post-war world would take the form of a battered but still autonomous Anglo–Soviet led Europe looking across the Atlantic to a financially supportive but politically distant USA. In fact, things turned out very differently. At some point – in and around the time of the Yalta Conference – the political situation was transformed. The Europe/America framework began to break down and the East/West configuration emerged.

### Examiners' notes

Each Section B question is accompanied by three sources that offer differences in their interpretations of the relevant controversy. To make the best use of these sources, first establish the interpretation that is being offered. For example, in Source 1, Harbutt argues that the origins of the Cold War can be traced back to the Yalta Conference.

## The Cold War begins, 1946–7

During 1946 and 1947, tensions between East and West grew. The mood changed as both sides increased propaganda attacks against each other, and prioritised domestic concerns over international co-operation.

### A 'war of words'

February 1946 marked the beginning of a 'war of words' between the USSR and the USA. Speaking at a meeting of the Supreme Soviet on 9 February, Stalin claimed that, in the long run, peace between capitalist and communist nations was impossible because capitalist competition inevitably led to war. This claim alarmed British and US ministers who considered the speech as an ideological attack on the capitalist West.

George Kennan, Deputy Head of the US mission in Moscow at the time, responded to Stalin's speech with the so-called 'Long Telegram'. This article argued that the USSR was building up its military power in order to spread communism across Europe, and that the USA should pursue a policy of containment. At the same time, the Soviet ambassador in Washington, Novikov, sent his own telegram to Stalin. Novikov's telegram argued that, after the death of Roosevelt, the USA had turned its back on co-operation and was starting a propaganda campaign to prepare the US public for a war against the USSR.

### The Iran Crisis, 1946

The Iran Crisis of March 1946 was significant, as it indicated to Britain and the USA that their fears were correct. It implied that the USSR was preparing to expand its influence. Moreover, it led to the final breakdown of the Grand Alliance.

Iran was occupied by Britain and the USSR during the Second World War. At the end of the war, the USSR occupied the north of Iran and Britain occupied the south. The USSR had agreed to withdraw its troops from the north by March 1946 and to hand over this territory to the British. However, by the end of March it was clear that the Soviets had no intention of withdrawing their troops. As a result, Britain and the USA united in condemnation of the USSR's 'aggressive imperialist policy'. The Iran Crisis led to a clear division within the Grand Alliance, between the USA and Britain on one hand, and the USSR on the other hand.

### Difficulties in Western Europe

Western Europe experienced severe economic difficulties from 1946 to 1947. A bad harvest, followed by a harsh winter, led to chronic food shortages in Germany. These problems were multiplied by the division of Europe, which stopped East–West trade in commodities such as grain. The economic hardship in Germany was major, and Western powers feared that these difficulties would discredit capitalism and lead to increased support for communism.

### The Iron Curtain, 1946

Churchill set out how the West viewed the USSR in his 'Iron Curtain' speech of March 1946. He argued that Europe had been divided by a metaphorical iron curtain, and that Soviet influence was increasing in the East. More worrying, was the USSR's policy of undermining governments in the West. Churchill feared that Stalin planned to stir up revolutions across Europe and win power through revolution rather than a traditional military campaign. Churchill called on Western nations to resist this.

> **Essential notes**
>
> Containment was a policy pursued by Truman's government in relation to the USSR. Essentially, while seeking to avoid war with the USSR, the policy meant that the USA was committed to stopping the spread of communism beyond Russia and Eastern Europe.

## The Truman Doctrine and Marshall Aid, 1947

In 1947, Truman outlined a new doctrine, coupled with an aid package, to prevent communism from spreading to Western Europe. Truman described the Truman Doctrine and Marshall Aid as 'two sides of the same walnut'.

## The significance of the Truman Doctrine and the Marshall Plan

The new policy of the USA was significant for the following reasons:

- It demonstrated that the USA's priority was to rebuild Western Europe, and not to co-operate with the USSR.

- The USSR believed that the Marshall Plan was an attempt to divide Europe into 'two camps'.

- The USSR pressurised countries in Eastern Europe to reject Marshall Aid by offering them the Molotov Plan of July 1947 instead.

- In September 1947, the USSR responded to developments in Western Europe by creating COMINFORM (the Communist Information Bureau), which imposed the USSR's control over significant aspects of government in Eastern Europe.

### The Truman Doctrine (March 1947)

The Truman Doctrine stated that:
- The world had become divided between communist tyranny and democratic freedom.
- The USA would fight for freedom wherever it was threatened.
- The USA would commit economic and military resources to help governments that were threatened by communism.
- Communism should be contained.

Truman Doctrine and the Marshall Plan: A package to contain communism

### The Marshall Plan (June 1947)

The Marshall Plan was intended to revive capitalism in Western Europe, and in so doing prevent Western Europe from coming under the influence of communism.
- Thirteen billion US dollars were to be used to rebuild Europe following the Second World War.
- To qualify for the money, nations must commit themselves to free trade.
- The USSR was unable to offer a similar aid package; therefore the Marshall Plan implicitly exposed the weakness of the Soviet economy.

### Essential notes

The Molotov Plan was a series of mutual trading agreements between the USSR and the communist states of Eastern Europe. The Plan formed the basis of COMECON (the Council for Mutual Economic Assistance), which was set up two years later.

### Source 2

(From John Young and John Kent, *International Relations Since 1945*, published by Oxford University Press 2004)

In 1946 suspicion and mistrust grew, even though, on both sides, there were still signs of willingness to compromise. In 1947, this willingness was to disappear and confrontation was, eventually, to lead to the end of efforts at co-operation. For both the USA and the USSR, 1947 was to be a crucial year. This was when fears of losing control over their respective European satellites or areas of influence reached such an extent that the two powers prioritised the consolidation of Europe into two opposing blocs. The key issues in the abandonment of co-operation were the failure to reach agreement on the future of Germany and discussions on the Marshall Plan, to provide American economic aid to Europe.

### Examiners' notes

Section B questions require you to integrate the sources' interpretations with your own knowledge of different interpretations of the controversy. Source 2 argues that even though there was 'willingness to compromise' in 1946, the Cold War emerged out of mutual suspicion. You could support this from your own knowledge of to the 'Long Telegram' and Novikov's telegram, which clearly provide evidence of mutual suspicion at the time.

German Democratic
Republic: October 1949

Poland:
January 1947

Czechoslovakia:
February 1948

Hungary:
August 1947

Albania:
January 1946

Romania:
February 1945

Bulgaria:
October 1946

The conversion of Eastern Europe to communism

### The Stalinisation of Eastern Europe, 1945–53

The US government believed that Stalin had a master plan for extending his influence over Eastern Europe. Yet, in 1945, the Russian government was divided over future relations with Eastern Europe:

- Georgi Malenkov, a senior member of the Russian government, argued that Russia should withdraw from Eastern Europe and focus on rebuilding its own industry.

- Maxim Litvinov, the former Russian Ambassador to the USA, argued that Russia should have a sphere of influence in Eastern Europe, including, at a minimum, Poland and Romania.

During 1945, Russia imposed a communist government in Romania. However, in Poland, Stalin guaranteed a government that was to be chosen by free election. Equally, in 1946, Hungary and Czechoslovakia proceeded with free elections. The difference in treatment is significant because it indicates that in the period immediately after the Second World War, Stalin had yet to formulate a consistent policy towards Eastern Europe.

**Essential notes**

A satellite state is a country that is officially independent; in practice it is controlled by another country.

### Satellite states

A consistent policy towards Eastern Europe emerged during 1947, after the USA offer of Marshall Aid.

Stalin regarded Marshall Aid as an attempt by the USA to build 'a Western Bloc' in Europe. He felt that he needed to tighten his control over Eastern Europe, which happened as follows:

- In August 1947, rigged elections led to the formation of a communist government in Hungary.

- Similarly, in February 1948, a communist coup in Czechoslovakia ousted the elected government, replacing it with a communist government.

By the end of 1949, the majority of Eastern Europe had become a series of Russian satellite states.

**Essential notes**

Expansionism describes the policy of a state that is determined to enlarge its territory or expand its sphere of influence.

### Western reaction

Truman was horrified by the extension of Soviet control in Eastern Europe. It confirmed his fears that Stalin was pursuing an expansionist policy that was designed to advance Communism, as Stalin had achieved this expansion through local Communist Parties rather than military action. Consequently, the Cold War deepened because of Truman's conviction that Stalin sought European domination.

### Germany and Berlin

At the end of the Second World War a series of unresolved questions relating to Germany remained:

- Politics – How would Germany be governed?

- Structure – Would Germany be united or divided?

- Reparations – Would Germany be forced to pay for war damages, and if so, how much?

- Borders – Where would Germany's borders with Poland lie?

In 1945, Germany, and its capital, Berlin, were divided into four zones, and administered by the four allies who had won the Second World War.

The division was intended to be temporary. However, negotiations among the four powers about the future of Germany were inconclusive.

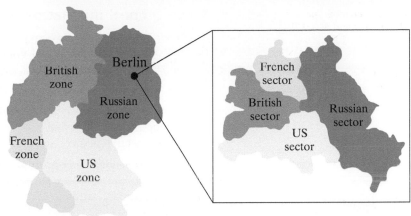

The division of Germany and Berlin

By 1947, the British, US and French zones, Trizonia, were working as a co-ordinated unit. As the Cold War deepened, negotiations between the West and Russia halted.

### The Berlin Blockade, 1948–9

Stalin responded to the increased co-ordination of West Germany by blockading Berlin; he cut off all routes to Berlin so that the Western zone was denied supplies. He was able to do this because Berlin was located in Soviet-administered East Germany. Stalin's intention was to force the Western powers to negotiate with him over the future of Germany, and if this could not be achieved, to claim the whole of Berlin for Russia.

### The Berlin airlift

Berlin became a symbol of Western resistance to Soviet expansion during the first part of the Cold War. It was also the first test of Truman's containment policy. Truman pledged to keep Berlin supplied by air. During the 324 days of the blockade, US and British planes ferried 13 000 tonnes of supplies to West Berlin.

The Berlin airlift was significant because:

- It demonstrated the commitment of the USA to fighting communism in Western Europe.

- It humiliated Stalin, forcing him to back down and end the blockade.

- It showed that Stalin was unwilling to engage the USA in military conflict, as he refused to shoot down American planes flying over Soviet-controlled airspace.

In addition, the failure of the Soviet blockade forced Stalin to recognise that he could not prevent the division of Germany. As a result, Germany was formally divided into the Federal Republic of Germany (West Germany) and the German Democratic Republic (East Germany).

### Examiners' notes

Some historians argue that as Marshall Aid led to the tightening of Soviet control over Eastern Europe, it was the major cause of the Cold War. Other historians dispute this, pointing to developments such as the Truman Doctrine, which they believe to be the true origin of the Cold War.

## The origins of the Korean War

In 1949, the USA suffered a series of setbacks. This meant that for the first time, the USSR was winning the Cold War.

- In August, the USSR successfully tested its first atomic bomb – three years ahead of expectations in the USA.

- In October, Mao Zedong proclaimed the creation of the People's Republic of China, marking a successful communist takeover of the world's most populous country.

US politicians believed that these two events showed that Truman had lost the initiative in the Cold War, and that the USA needed to take a tougher stance in its conflict with Russia.

### NSC-68

Under pressure from Congress, Truman and senior government officials began to rethink their approach to the Cold War. Truman's new policy towards Russia was set out in a secret document known as NSC-68, written in early 1950. NSC-68 addressed how the USA saw the world, and how Truman planned to respond to the Soviet threat.

| NSC-68 | |
|---|---|
| How the USA saw the world | The US government believed that, after the Second World War, the world had become bipolar. |
| | The USSR was aiming at world domination – starting its campaign in Europe and Asia. |
| | The USA had slashed military expenditure since 1945, creating a real imbalance with the USSR, who continued to spend lavishly. For example, in 1948, the USA spent $10.9 billion in contrast to the USSR's $13.1 billion; the USA had 640 000 in the army, and one armoured division, whereas the USSR had 2.6 million in the army and 30 armoured divisions. |
| How the USA would respond to the Soviet threat | The USA had a responsibility to provide an alternative political and economic model to that of communism. |
| | The USA should be prepared to engage in limited wars in order to resist communism and advance US aims. |
| | The USSR must be handled forcefully and negotiation was only possible from a position of US strength. |
| | The USA should increase military spending and develop a hydrogen bomb to regain the initiative in the arms race. |
| | US power should be used to contain and, where possible, 'roll back' communism. |

NSC-68 was significant because it showed that the USA was determined to be more aggressive in its approach towards the USSR.

**Essential notes**

NSC-68 stands for National Security Council Report 68. The National Security Council was set up in 1947 by President Truman in order to develop Cold War policy.

**Essential notes**

The phrase 'bipolar world' emerged during the Cold War to describe the relationship between the superpowers and their allies. It suggested that smaller countries would be drawn to one or other of the superpowers, which were comparable to the poles of a magnet.

**Essential notes**

The phrase 'arms race' refers to competition over the size and sophistication of the superpowers' military resources.

**Source 3**
(From Campbell Craig and Fredrik Logewall, *America's Cold War: the Politics of Insecurity,* published by The Belknap Press 2009)

For all of the expansive and universalistic rhetoric of NSC-68, the position of its authors on the new realities established by the Soviet [atomic] bomb was clear: the primary purpose of the United States must now be to wage the Cold war without getting into an atomic war, and without having to concede to Soviet demands to avoid one.

## Causes of the Korean War

The long-term, medium-term and short-term causes of the Korean War are listed in the columns below:

| Long-term causes | Medium-term causes | Short-term causes |
| --- | --- | --- |
| Between 1910 and 1945, Korea was controlled by Japan. | By 1949, the South Korean government of Syngman Rhee appeared extremely vulnerable: | In 1950, the USA refused to give aid and military assistance to South Korea. This convinced Kim Il-Sung that the USA would not stop a communist invasion of South Korea. |
| Following the defeat of Japan at the end of the Second World War, Korea was divided into a Soviet zone in the North, and a US zone in the South. | • It was unpopular with the South Korean people.<br>• It relied heavily on the support of US troops. | Kim Il-Sung persuaded Stalin to agree to a North Korean invasion of South Korea. |
| In the context of the Cold War, agreement between the USA and the USSR on the future of Korea was impossible. Therefore Korea remained divided. | In 1949, the USA and the USSR agreed to withdraw their troops from Korea. This led Kim Il-Sung, the leader of North Korea, to believe that the South Korean government could be overthrown with ease. | |

With Stalin's backing, Kim Il-Sung ordered his troops to invade South Korea on June 25, 1950.

**Source 4**
(From Jussi M. Hanhimäki and Odd Arne Westad, *The Cold War,* published by Oxford University Press 2004)

The war that followed the North Korean attack on South Korea in June 1950 was the first 'hot' war of the Cold War era, and perhaps its most dangerous conflict in terms of superpower involvement. The war signalled a new level of permanent tension between East and West … It also told Moscow and Beijing that the United States was ready to fight a war on the East-Asian mainland against the expansion of Soviet rule.

**Examiners' notes**

It is important that you use your own knowledge to help you understand the meaning of the sources. At first glance, the final part of Source 3 seems to suggest that the USSR wanted to avoid an atomic war. However, your own knowledge should help you to interpret the source. NSC-68 was a US document, so the source is referring to the US desire to avoid atomic war.

**Examiners' notes**

Section B questions require you to integrate material from a range of sources. To do this effectively, you must understand how the sources agree and how they differ in their interpretations. For example, consider the question, 'How far do you agree that the development of the Soviet nuclear bomb in 1949 marked the beginning of a new era in the Cold War?' If you were given sources 3 and 4 to help you, you would need to consider the following in your essay:

• Both sources agree that a new era of the Cold War began in the period 1949–50.
• However, the sources differ about the cause of this new era. Source 3 attributes the cause to the Soviet atomic bomb. Source 4, however, blames the Korean War for the new phase.

## Essential notes

In order to involve the UN in the Korean War, Truman needed the approval of the UN Security Council. The USSR was a member of the Security Council and was expected to veto UN involvement in the war. However, the USSR was boycotting the UN in protest to their refusal to recognise Mao's China, and therefore played no part in the vote.

## Examiners' notes

You can use relevant own knowledge to elaborate on the information provided in the sources in order to answer the Section B question. For example, if using Source 5, you could provide the following details from your own knowledge:

- the nature of Mao's regime in China
- the reasons for Soviet and Chinese support for North Korea
- the reasons for UN intervention in Korea
- the impact made by the intervention of Chinese troops.

# The Korean War, 1950–53

## US reaction to the outbreak of war in Korea

For American politicians, Kim Il-Sung's invasion of South Korea was evidence of Communist desire for world domination. Congress already blamed President Truman for doing too little during the Cold War, so he was under huge pressure to stand up to communism in Korea. Truman responded by appealing to the United Nations (UN). He hoped that a UN force would have more authority than a purely US force because it represented the international community, not just the USA. As a result, the UN despatched an international force that was headed by the US General, Douglas MacArthur.

## The impact of the Korean War on superpower relations

The Korean War was significant for the development of the Cold War in the following ways:

- It marked a shift of focus in the Cold War, from Europe to Asia.

- The Armistice was signed following Stalin's death in 1953. Although Russia had not participated in the war, North Korea and China were fighting with Stalin's explicit approval. The Armistice indicated that the new generation of Soviet leaders were prepared to pursue a less confrontational relationship with the USA.

- The war was a partial success for both sides:

  - The USA had contained communism, but failed to roll it back.

  - The US government used communist aggression in Korea to justify military spending, one of its major policy initiatives. Indeed, military spending increased threefold between 1950 and 1955.

  - The communist powers had reasserted control over North Korea, but had failed to extend their territory.

### Source 5
(From Robert J. McMahon, *The Cold War: A Very Short Introduction*, published by Oxford University Press 2003)

[By 1950] the world faced an entirely new Cold War ... one whose boundaries reached well beyond Europe. The emergence of Mao's regime in China, the Sino–Soviet alliance, Soviet and Chinese support for North Korean adventurism, the intervention of US and UN forces in Korea, the subsequent entry of Chinese troops ... all ensured that the Cold War would remain the commanding presence in postwar Asia for a long time to come.

**Phase 1: June–August 1950**
The North Korean army pushed south and captured Seoul, the capital of South Korea.

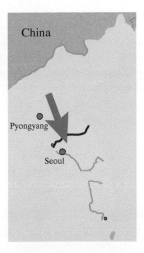

**Phase 2: September 1950**
In early September, MacArthur and the UN forces landed in South Korea. By the end of September, the UN forces have pushed the North Korean Army back to the 38th Parallel, the border between North and South Korea.

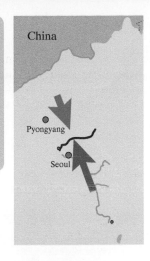

**Phase 3: September–November 1950**
Between September and November, the UN forces 'rolled back' the North Korean forces, capturing Pyongyang, the capital of North Korea, in October, and heading for the Yalu River (the border, with China).

**Phase 4: November–December 1950**
In November 1950, China entered the Korean War fighting for North Korea. Mao feared that the UN would invade China if they successfully defeated North Korea. A combined force of 350 000 communist troops pushed the UN back to the 38th Parallel.

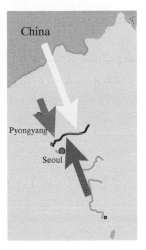

**Phase 5: January 1951–July 1953**
The fighting continued for the next two years, but essentially the two sides had reached a stalemate. MacArthur advised Truman to use nuclear weapons against China. Truman refused, fearing that it would lead to nuclear retaliation by the USSR. The two sides signed an Armistice in July 1953, bringing the conflict to an end.
Korea remained divided.

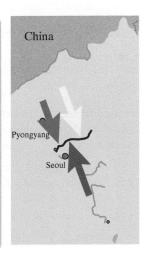

The course of the Korean War in five phases

### Examiners' notes

Here you need to:

- grasp how capitalism and communism gave rise to competing US and Soviet views of the post-war order, which generated tension
- identify the strengths and weaknesses of this perspective, because this will help you to evaluate the 'ideological confrontation' interpretation in the actual exam.

Evaluation is a high-level skill and will gain you marks.

### Examiners' notes

Section B questions require you to extract relevant material to develop source-based arguments. For example, if you were answering the question, 'To what extent was the development of the Cold War in the years 1945 to 1953 due to US–Soviet ideological rivalry?', you could use the following points from Source 6:

- Their respective ideologies gave the USA and the USSR a deeply held conviction that they were to play a global role after 1945.
- Both saw their ideological perspective as the route to a better world.
- Their ideologies were diametrically opposed and were bound to lead to US–Soviet conflict.

## Ideological confrontation

Ideological confrontation between the Soviet Union and the USA was central to the development of the Cold War. This is not surprising, since US–Soviet ideological differences stretched back to the 1917 Bolshevik Revolution, when Russia became the first Marxist state. Historian Robert J. McMahon has neatly summarised how the competing claims of capitalism and communism helped to generate US-Soviet rivalry:

> **Source 6**
> (From Robert J. McMahon, *The Cold War: A Very Short Introduction*, published by Oxford University Press 2003)
>
> Ideology imparted to Soviets and Americans alike, a messianic faith in the world historical roles of their respective nations. On each side of the Cold War divide, leaders and ordinary citizens saw their countries acting for much broader purposes than the mere advancement of national interests. Soviets and Americans each saw themselves acting out of noble motives to usher humanity into a grand new age of peace, justice and order. Married to the overwhelming power that each nation possessed, at a time when much of the world lay prostrate, those mirror-opposite ideological values provided a sure-fire recipe for conflict.

### The impact of Communist ideology on the development of the Cold War 1945–53

Orthodox, or traditional, historians have argued that the USSR's adherence or loyalty to communism was the vital factor in the development of the Cold War from 1945 to 1953. According to this view, conflict with the USA was inevitable, given the Soviet regime's:

- commitment to the Marxist-Leninist doctrine of class struggle
- promotion of communist revolution on a global scale
- fundamental hostility towards the capitalist states, particularly the USA and Britain.

The impact of communist ideology on the Cold War between 1945 and 1953 is examined in the diagram opposite.

### *Orthodox interpretation of the development of the Cold War*

The orthodox interpretation of the development of the Cold War emphasises the following points:

- The USSR was responsible for the Cold War because it was motivated by communism, an expansionist and anti-capitalist ideology, that advocated global revolution.

- This ideological stance led the Soviet Union to become aggressively expansionist (for example, in Eastern Europe) in order to extend Communist power and undermine capitalism.

- In turn, this compelled the USA to adopt a policy of containment (such as the Truman Doctrine, the Marshall Plan and the formation of NATO – the North Atlantic Treaty Organisation – to prevent the spread of communism and to defend capitalism and thus 'freedom').

The orthodox interpretation has been supported by historians such as William H. McNeill, Herbert Feis and Arthur M. Schlesinger Jr.

**Several of the USSR's actions in Europe can be seen as being motivated by a desire to spread communism:**
- The 'Stalinisation' of Poland, Bulgaria, Hungary, Romania and East Germany between 1945 and 1947
- The communist coup in Czechoslovakia (1948)
- The Berlin Blockade of 1948–9

**Soviet co-ordination and control of the wider communist movement**
The COMINFORM (1947) was an instrument designed to increase Soviet control over other Communist Parties. Many viewed it as a revamped COMINTERN – an organisation to promote worldwide communist revolution. COMECON (1949) was a Soviet-dominated agency, which co-ordinated and controlled economic development in the Eastern Bloc.

**The impact of communist ideology on the development of the Cold War, 1945–53**

**Communist expansion in Asia**
- Mao's assumption of power in China (1949) held out the prospect of a monolithic Communist Bloc across Eurasia.
- The USSR approved communist North Korea's attack on pro-western South Korea (1950). The Soviets also supplied the North with weapons and military advisers. China committed some 400 000 troops to the North-Korean cause.

**Soviet encouragement of left-wing dissent in non-communist countries**
Under Soviet instructions, the French and Italian Communist Parties began a 'destabilisation' campaign of strikes and demonstrations in their respective countries (1947–8) against the Marshall Plan. Some two million French workers were involved in this anti-capitalist protest.

The impact of communist ideology on the development of the Cold War, 1945–53

Continued on the next two pages

## Impact of capitalist ideology on the development of the Cold War

Rejecting orthodox anti-communist interpretations, revisionist historians have maintained that the USA's policy of capitalist expansion was the key element in the development of the Cold War from 1945 to 1953. From this perspective, America's post-war capitalist aims made conflict with the Soviet Union inevitable:

- The US intended to impose a 'Pax Americana' as a global peace settlement.

- Attempts to open up particularly sensitive areas to US economic activity (such as Eastern Europe) were bound to be resisted by the USSR.

- The USA, as the leading capitalist power, was strongly anti-communist.

The impact of capitalist ideology on the Cold War between 1945 and 1953 is examined in the diagram below:

**The US drive for markets after 1945**
- The expanding US capitalist community needed ever-increasing trade and investment opportunities abroad because American markets could not absorb the nation's productive capacity. This implied growing US political influence across the globe.
- This so-called 'open-door policy', which was based on free trade and the removal of protectionism, favoured 'equal opportunity' in all foreign markets. However, given the enormous economic power of the USA, this could only lead to American international domination.
- The US 'military-industrial complex' had a vested interest in promoting a Cold War, partly to ensure continued high demand for the weapons produced by American arms companies.

**Early US attempts to force the USSR to accept an 'open-door' policy in Eastern Europe:**
- Lend-lease was ended abruptly (1945).
- The US refused to agree on German reparations (1945).
- The US tried to use nuclear monopoly as a negotiating tool (for example, Potsdam).
- The US ended reparations from the US German zone (1946).

**The impact of capitalist ideology on the development of the Cold War, 1945–53**

**The USA had the post-war confidence to shape the world according to American values:**
- US war losses were light – only 0.9% of its population.
- US industrial capacity increased by 90% (1940–44) and the USA produced 50% of the world's goods.
- America had a nuclear monopoly until 1949.

**An informal US empire in Europe**
The Marshall Plan can be seen as an example of US 'dollar-imperialism'. From this perspective, the Marshall Plan was an important part of the US strategy to mould post-war Europe into a capitalist bloc and detach the East European states from the USSR by offering them economic incentives.

## *Revisionist interpretation of the development of the Cold War*

The revisionist interpretation of the development of the Cold War emphasises the following points:

- The USA was responsible for the Cold War because it was motivated by capitalist expansion and the pursuit of global markets to maintain economic growth and avoid recession.
- This ideological stance led the USA to attempt to open other parts of the world to American trade and investment (such as the Marshall Plan in Europe) to extend US-dominated capitalist power and undermine communism.
- The threat of US economic imperialism compelled the USSR to consolidate the Soviet Bloc in Eastern Europe during the mid- to late-1940s in order to prevent capitalist infiltration of its sphere of influence.
- The USSR had been seriously weakened by the Second World War and was in no position to pursue world revolution or aggressive expansionism. From 1945 its main concerns were security and economic reconstruction.

The revisionist interpretation has been supported by historians such as William A. Williams, Lloyd C. Gardner and Gabriel Kolko.

### Ideological confrontation interpretation: an assessment

| Strengths | • Identifies the important role played by ideological commitment in promoting Cold War tensions from 1945<br>• Points out that US–Soviet ideological differences were long-standing and went back to the 1917 Bolshevik Revolution<br>• Highlights a fundamental difference of world-view between the two major powers<br>• Shows how USA and USSR national interests were often conceived in ideological terms, for example, US motives for offering Marshall Aid |
|---|---|
| Weaknesses | • Orthodox and revisionist explanations are one-sided in the sense that they over-estimate ideological motives and they understate the significance of Stalin and Truman's pragmatic reaction to circumstances<br>• Underestimates the importance of misperception and misjudgement in the development of the Cold War<br>• Not all Soviet or US actions were ideologically driven. Indeed, sometimes the leaders acted in a way that contradicted their ideology, for example, Stalin's refusal to support the Greek communists, which resulted in military setbacks |

### Examiners' notes

Here you need to:

- understand the key features of the ideological confrontation interpretation of the development of the Cold War from 1945 to 1953
- identify the strengths and weaknesses of this perspective.

**Examiners' notes**

Here you need to:

- understand the key features of the traditional great power rivalry interpretation of the development of the Cold War 1945–53 (students often confuse this interpretation with 'ideological confrontation', but examiners expect you to be able to distinguish between them)
- identify the strengths and weaknesses of this perspective.

**Essential notes**

Geopolitical inevitability in this context means that the expansion of US and Russian political and economic influence made conflict between the two powers unavoidable, irrespective of their ideologies or systems of government.

**Essential notes**

De Tocqueville (1805–59), a liberal, made this famous prediction in his best-known work *Democracy in America*, which was published in two volumes in 1835 and 1840.

Adolf Hitler also argued that conflict between the US and the USSR was inevitable. In 1945 he claimed 'there remain only two Great Powers capable of confronting each other – the United States and Soviet Russia. The laws of both history and geography will compel these two powers to a trial of strength, either military or in the fields of economics and ideology.'

## Traditional great power rivalry

Some historians argue that the Cold War was due to traditional great power rivalry. This view is based on several important factors that contributed to the deteriorating US–Soviet relationship after 1945, including:

- the geopolitical inevitability of US–Soviet conflict
- traditional Russian expansionism
- US interventionism
- the international situation in 1945.

### *Traditional great power rivalry interpretation of the development of the Cold War*

The traditional great power rivalry interpretation of the development of the Cold War emphasises the following points:

- During the First and Second World Wars, Britain and France attempted to maintain the status quo against the challenge of Germany. To do this, they had to rely on support from the dominant Western power, the USA. The Cold War essentially repeated this pattern with the new challenge coming from the USSR.

- Soviet foreign policy was driven by a deeply ingrained traditional Russian sense of fear and insecurity, which encouraged defensive expansion, understandable since Russia had been invaded in 1606, 1812, 1915, 1918 and 1941.

- The power vacuums created by the impact of the Second World War drew the two most powerful states – the USA and the USSR – into these areas in an attempt to extend their influence. US–Soviet conflict flowed from this.

The traditional great power rivalry interpretation is supported in the work of historians such as Louis J. Halle, Walter LaFeber and Thomas G. Paterson.

### Geopolitical inevitability

In 1835, the French political commentator Alexis de Tocqueville argued that the USA and Russia each seemed 'marked out by the will of Heaven to sway the destinies of half the globe'. From this perspective the Cold War was the inevitable outcome of the two powers' struggle for influence and prestige. Indeed, US and Russian expansionism, which pre-dated 1945, brought the two powers into closer contact, so generating rivalry. Historian Walter LaFeber supports this geopolitical argument:

**Source 7**

(From Walter LaFeber, *America, Russia and the Cold War 1945–1992*, published by McGraw-Hill 1993)

That conflict did not begin in 1945, or even in 1917. The two powers did not initially come into conflict because one was communist and the other capitalist. Rather, they first confronted each other on the plains of Asia in the late 19th century. That meeting climaxed a century in which Americans had expanded westward over half the globe and Russians had moved eastward across Asia.

## Traditional Russian expansionism

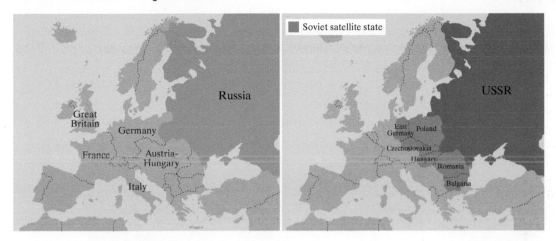

Left, the Tsarist Empire c.1914, and right, the Soviet Bloc c.1953

Some historians argue that the Cold War was a part of a long history of Russian expansionism. According to this view, Stalin's foreign policy, the prime cause of the Cold War, was essentially a continuation of the traditional expansionist objectives of the Tsarist Empire rather than an attempt to spread communism across the globe. Thus, Stalin acted as a 'Red Tsar' after 1945 by seeking to extend the Soviet Union's borders and influence. In this sense he was continuing Russia's 19th century policy of extending its territory by incorporating Poland into its empire and attempted to exercise dominance over the Balkans and the Middle East. One of Stalin's key post-war objectives, and a source of tension with the Western Powers, was to recover former Russian territory such as parts of Poland and the Baltic states, which had been lost under the Brest-Litovsk Treaty (1918).

Louis J. Halle has made this point:

### Source 8
(From Louis J. Halle, *The Cold War as History*, published by Harper & Row 1971)

Under the communists, Russia has continued to behave essentially as it behaved under the Czars. There has been the same conspiratorial approach to international relations ... the same profound mistrust of the outside world ... the same obsession with secrecy and espionage ... There has been the same effort to achieve security by expanding Russian space, by constantly pushing back the menacing presence of foreigners across Russian borders. What the revolution of 1917 did was simply to reinvigorate the traditional principle of authoritarianism.

In essence, Halle argues that Russia's communists continued important aspects of Tsarism such as authoritarianism and the desire to expand its influence and territory through underhand diplomacy. In this sense, he suggests that the Cold War was the outcome of Russia's ongoing desire to increase its influence and territory.

### Examiners' notes
Source 7 highlights three important points in the traditional great power rivalry argument:

- US–Russian rivalry pre-dated the 1917 Bolshevik Revolution
- this rivalry was not originally based on capitalist communist differences
- it emerged during the late 19th century as both powers sought to extend their political and economic influence in the same area – Asia.

### Examiners' notes
In Source 8, Halle makes the 'traditional great power rivalry' point that there was a good deal of continuity in the Russian approach to foreign affairs under Tsarist and Soviet systems, particularly with regard to secretive methods, seeking security through expansion and authoritarian policy-making.

## Essential notes

Interventionism means
one nation interfering, or
becoming involved, in the
affairs of another nation.

## US interventionism

The US policy of interventionism in European affairs has also been
suggested as a cause of the Cold War. The US interest in Europe following
1945 was part of a broader trend.

In the first half of the 20th century the major powers concluded that
control of the area between Central Europe and the Caucasus would bring
global dominance.

The USA had twice intervened in Europe, during the two World Wars, to
prevent Germany from dominating this region.

Franklin D. Roosevelt during his presidency

President Roosevelt publicly justified US involvement thus: 'If Great Britain
goes down, the Axis powers will control Europe, Asia, Africa, Australasia
and the high seas – and they will be in a position to bring enormous
military and naval resources against this hemisphere.' A similar argument
was used to justify US intervention to stop Soviet domination of Europe
after the Second World War. In this sense some historians argue that the
Cold War was caused by US intervention to counter the Soviet threat in
Europe after 1945.

## The international situation in 1945

Several historians, for example Thomas G. Paterson in *On Every Front: The Making and Unmaking of the Cold War* (1992), have emphasised that the impact of the Second World War on the international system made conflict between the USA and the USSR likely for a number of reasons:

- Redistribution of power:
  - the defeat of Germany, Italy and Japan left a power vacuum in Europe and Asia
  - British and French power was much reduced
  - the multipolar system of the 1930s had effectively collapsed.
- The USA and the USSR emerged from the Second World War as the two most powerful nations in a new bipolar system.
- The Second World War accelerated the disintegration of the European empires. As a result, former colonies became independent. However, the disintegration of the old Empires led to political instability, as the USA and the USSR competed for influence over the newly independent states. In this sense the Cold War emerged from the instabilities of the post-war world.

### Essential notes

A multipolar international system has several centres of power. In the 1930s, Britain, France, Germany, the USA and the USSR could all claim to be great powers.

In a bipolar international system, such as existed from 1945, two states possess most of the political, economic, military and cultural influence.

## Traditional great power rivalry interpretation: an assessment

| Strengths | Takes a long-term view by connecting the development of the Cold War to well-established trends in US and Russian foreign policy |
| --- | --- |
| | Identifies the role of traditional national self-interest in promoting Cold War tensions |
| | Highlights how the destabilising effects of the Second World War encouraged US–Soviet rivalry |
| Weaknesses | Underestimates the ideological causes of the Cold War |
| | US–Soviet antagonism can be seen as a new type of great power rivalry, because, by the 1950s it had assumed a truly global scale |
| | Unlike previous great power confrontations, US–Soviet rivalry did not result in direct war because of the development of nuclear weapons |

# Responsibility of the leaders: Roosevelt and Truman

## Personal responsibility for the Cold War

Important factors such as ideological differences and great power rivalry certainly contributed to the development of the Cold War but it 'took men, responding unpredictably to circumstances, to forge the chain of causation' (John Lewis Gaddis, *We Now Know*, 1997). In other words, the personalities, outlooks and decisions of the American, Soviet and British leaders had a significant impact.

## Roosevelt

Roosevelt, who had first been elected President in 1932, dominated US politics until early 1945. His role at the Yalta Conference (February 1945), however, has sharply divided opinion.

| Roosevelt: Naïve or shrewd at Yalta? | |
|---|---|
| **Naïve** | **Shrewd** |
| • Roosevelt (and Churchill) made too many concessions to the USSR over Poland and China. | • Roosevelt (and Churchill) recognised the 'hard realities of power' – by the end of the war the USSR would be in a strong position in Europe and Asia. |
| • Duped by Stalin over free elections in Poland | • Flexible over Poland, mainly because the Red Army had already occupied the country |
| • May have suffered from mental impairment at the conference, which led to poor decision-making | • Concluded that Western concessions to the Soviet Union were necessary to ensure that the allies successfully concluded the war in Europe together |
| • 'Wrote off' Eastern Europe as a Soviet sphere of influence and therefore effectively encouraged Communist expansion | • the USSR then entered the campaign against Japan enduring US–Soviet co-operation would become the cornerstone of stable post-war order |
| • Afterwards, acknowledged that Stalin was already exploiting or disregarding various arrangements made at Yalta | • Secured important gains at Yalta – Soviet involvement in the UN, the USSR's pledge to fight Japan, and Stalin's recognition of the pro-US Nationalist Chinese regime |
| | • His death removed the Western leader who might have succeeded in extending US-Soviet co-operation into the post-war period |

**Source 9**
(From Richard Crockatt, *The United States and the Cold War 1941–53*, published by the British Association for American Studies 1989)

Even before FDR's death on 8 April 1945 wrangles had developed over the observance of the [Polish] agreement, as the Soviet Union made it clear that it was unprepared either to accord non-communists any real role or to conduct the kind of elections which would satisfy the West.

**Source 10**
(From Robert Dallek, *Franklin D. Roosevelt and American Foreign Policy, 1932–45*, published by Oxford University Press 1979)

On all the central issues [discussed at Yalta] – the United Nations, Germany, Poland, Eastern Europe, and the Far East – Roosevelt largely followed through on earlier plans and gained most of what he wished: the world body, the division of Germany, the pronouncement on Poland, and the Declaration on Liberated Europe promised to encourage American involvement abroad and possible long-term accommodation with the USSR.

## Truman

Roosevelt's successor, the more anti-communist Harry Truman, introduced a much harder edge to US Cold War diplomacy after April 1945. Consequently, Truman's elevation to the Presidency has generally been regarded as a significant factor in the development of the Cold War. It certainly put Truman on a steep learning curve and he admitted that 'I feel like I've been struck by a bolt of lightning'.

Truman could not match Roosevelt's charisma and public speaking skills. He also lacked the social and intellectual confidence of his more affluent and well-connected predecessor. These limitations led to a deep-seated inferiority complex. Truman's uncompromising anti-communist stance undoubtedly increased Soviet fears and made Stalin less likely to co-operate.

In May 1945, Truman wrote in a private note 'I've no faith in any totalitarian state. They all start with the wrong premise – that lies are justified and the end justifies the means. But Russian Godless Pervert Systems won't work'. Some of the key influences on Truman's leadership are shown in the diagram below.

**Examiners' notes**

Sources 9 and 10 are similar to the types of sources you are likely to encounter in the exam. Read them carefully, as they should be cross-referenced to develop a support/challenge approach. For example, Dallek's positive assessment of the Yalta statement on Poland can be challenged with Crockatt's argument that the USSR quickly disregarded this. You would, of course, need to bring in your own knowledge as well.

**Containment of the Soviet Union**
- Truman quickly became convinced that the USSR was an expansionist power, which the USA had to contain.
- He consciously developed a 'get tough' policy to try to stem communist growth, for example, he:
  – upbraided Molotov over Soviet policy on Poland (1945)
  – used US nuclear monopoly to put pressure on Stalin at Potsdam (1945)
  – ran supply flights to thwart the Berlin Blockade (1948–9).

**Personal characteristics and beliefs**
- Truman was stridently anti-communist and more suspicious of Soviet motives than Roosevelt.
- He tended to see issues in black and white terms and had an 'us' and 'them' world view.
- He lacked the patience to work through complex problems. Truman admitted he was not up on all details.

**Truman's conduct of the Cold War, 1945–53**

**Lack of international experience**
- Roosevelt did not keep Truman informed as Vice-President. They had only two private meetings before Roosevelt's death.
- Truman had little prior knowledge of foreign affairs.
- His inexperience made him keen to establish a strong international reputation.

**Talking up the Soviet threat**
Truman deliberately exaggerated the communist threat to secure key objectives such as:
- Congressional aid to Greece and Turkey
- US acceptance of the Truman Doctrine.

**Domestic pressures**
As President of a liberal democracy, Truman had to take US public and political opinion into account. For example, his decision to intervene in Korea (1950) was partly influenced by domestic criticism, that his government had 'lost' China in 1949.

## Examiners' notes

Here you need to:

- understand the extent to which Churchill and Stalin were responsible for the development of the Cold War 1945–53. (Stalin's motives were not always clear, which is why historians interpret his actions in different ways)
- identify the strengths and weaknesses of this perspective (do you find this approach more or less convincing to explain the onset of the Cold War?).

## Essential notes

In a meeting with Stalin (October 1944), Churchill produced a note outlining post-war spheres of influence in terms of agreement of percentages:

- Romania (90% Russian, 10% British)
- Greece (90% British–American, 10% Russian)
- Yugoslavia and Hungary (50:50 split between Russia and Western allies)
- Bulgaria (75% Russian, 25% British–American).

Stalin ticked the note.

# Responsibility of the leaders: Churchill and Stalin

## Churchill

By 1945 Britain was very much the second Western power after the USA. Churchill's actions also had an impact on the developing Cold War:

- Deeply anti-communist, Churchill had called for foreign intervention against the Bolsheviks in 1918, so Stalin never really trusted him. In fact the Soviet leader remarked in 1944 that 'Churchill is the kind who, if you don't watch him, will slip a kopeck [a Russian coin] out of your pocket'. Churchill's view of the USSR was equally suspicious: 'Trying to maintain good relations is like wooing a crocodile. You do not know whether to tickle it under the chin or to beat it over the head. When it opens its mouth you cannot tell whether it is trying to smile or prepare to eat you up'.

- In October 1944, Churchill drew up the 'percentages agreement' with Stalin. This gave Stalin the impression that a post-war Soviet sphere of influence in Eastern Europe had unspoken Western approval.

- Churchill's 'Iron Curtain' speech (March 1946) sharpened East–West divisions. Truman was delighted with Churchill's uncompromising anti-Soviet statement, but Stalin condemned the speech as war-mongering and compared the British wartime leader to Hitler.

### Source 11

(From Jeremy Isaacs and Taylor Downing, *The Cold War*, published by Little, Brown 2008)

In an address at Westminster College in Fulton [Missouri], on 5 March 1946, Churchill articulated in public what was being said privately in Washington: 'From Stettin in the Baltic to Trieste in the Adriatic, an iron curtain has descended across the continent.'

But American opinion was not yet ready for this strong attack on a wartime ally. Churchill's speech was thought at the time to be too extreme, and most of the press denounced it. Even Truman, who had known beforehand of its content, had to say he had not; when pressed for a reaction at the time, he declined to comment.

## Stalin

Stalin's character and actions have been examined by historians seeking to explain the development of the Cold War. Few would dispute that Stalin played a major role in the deteriorating East–West relationship. Many have argued that Stalin's overriding goals were:

- security through expansion
- consolidation of a Soviet sphere of influence.

It would also seem to be the case that the Soviet leader had a flexible approach to achieving these goals. In their competing explanations, historians have emphasised different aspects of his leadership as being contributory factors to the development of the Cold War.

These include his dysfunctional personality, his preoccupation with Soviet security (misconstrued, or misinterpreted, by the West), his role as an expansionist communist and his pursuit of flawed policies.

Some of the key features of Stalin's leadership are shown below:

**Personality**
- Suspicious and secretive
- Cunning
- Authoritarian
- Deeply xenophobic
- No moral qualms about using terror and violence
- The need to be respected and feared
- Naturally averse to conciliation and compromise

**Preoccupation with Soviet security**
- Russia had been invaded in 1915, 1918 and 1941. Understandably, Stalin was preoccupied with Soviet security.
- His policy on Poland (1945) and the 'Stalinisation' of Eastern Europe (1945–8) reflected a genuine desire to protect the USSR from any future Western attack by creating a defensive buffer zone.
- On various occasions, Stalin exercised caution and restraint, for example:
  – He recognised Greece as an area of British influence.
  – He did not object to US troops being stationed in South Korea (1945–9) despite its proximity to the USSR.

**Promoting Cold War tension**
Stalin also promoted Cold War tension to defend, and gain popular approval for his domestic policies. In a February 1946 speech, for example, Stalin warned the USSR of the danger of a future war waged by the capitalist powers. He did this to justify the introduction of three further Five-Year Plans to strengthen the Soviet economy.

**Aggressive and expansionist**
- Attempted to retain a presence in Iran after the war to secure access to oil supplies.
- Aimed to extend the USSR's influence into Southern Europe: Stalin put pressure on Turkey to try to establish Soviet control over the Dardanelles.
- In 1947, Stalin remarked that if Churchill had delayed the second front by a year, 'the Red Army would have come to France … [we] toyed with the idea of reaching Paris.'
For other examples, see also 'Ideological confrontation' on p. 16.

**Stalin's mistakes**
Several of Stalin's policies were flawed and increased Cold War divisions, for example:
- The Berlin Blockade (1948–9) was ill-conceived because it led to the creation of a capitalist West Germany and the NATO military alliance.
- Stalin's support for North Korea's attack on the South (1950) failed to recognise the USA's determination to defend South Korea or that the West would respond rapidly.

**Wary of the West**
Stalin was suspicious of the West because of:
- Western hostility to the 1917 Revolution and intervention in the Russian Civil War
- Allied delays in opening up a second front in Europe during the Second World War
- Other 'unfriendly' acts such as the abrupt end of lend-lease (1945), Soviet exclusion from the post-war administration of Japan, and US refusal to share nuclear secrets.

## Leaders' responsibility interpretation: an assessment

| | |
|---|---|
| **Strengths** | Focuses on the key individuals who took the major decisions in the years 1945–1953, which led to the Cold War |
| | Approach is particularly valuable in examining Soviet behaviour, bearing in mind Stalin's uniquely powerful position within the USSR |
| | Can also reveal the constraints and pressures under which the national leaders had to operate during the early stages of the Cold War |
| **Weaknesses** | Personality-based explanations may exaggerate the importance of a key individual in the developing Cold War |
| | Such an approach may underestimate the relative importance of structural factors such as ideological differences and traditional great power rivalry |

## Essential notes

The post-revisionist interpretation of the development of the Cold War emphasises the following points:

- The superpowers' competing interests, their misperceptions and the vicious circle of superpower action and reaction that shaped US–Soviet relations after the Second World War.
- The USSR's understandable desire for security and its traditional suspicion of the West led to exaggerated Western fears about Soviet expansionism and the USSR's military strength. Stalin's posturing and aggressive behaviour (in fact more a sign of Soviet weakness than strength) reinforced Western concerns.
- Within the Soviet Bloc, Stalin greatly exaggerated the Western military threat. President Truman's tougher policy towards the USSR appeared to support the Soviet leader's claims.

The post-revisionist interpretation has been supported by historians such as John Lewis Gaddis, Melvyn P. Leffler and Martin McCauley.

# Misjudgement and misperception

## The post-revisionist approach

Post-revisionist historians tend to dismiss orthodox and revisionist explanations of the development of the Cold War on the grounds that they:

- are highly partisan – either pro-American or pro-Soviet
- oversimplify a complex historical process.

Post-revisionists tend to avoid placing the blame on one superpower or the other. Instead, they emphasise that US–USSR relations deteriorated due to the interaction of various factors, which led to misjudgement and misperception on both sides. Some of the key post-revisionist arguments regarding the US–USSR relationship between 1945 and 1953 are highlighted in the following lists.

## USA – Misjudgements and misperceptions

| |
|---|
| Since the USA had no neighbouring enemy and had not been invaded since the 19th century, the American government was not well placed to empathise with the Soviets' deep sense of insecurity in 1945. |
| The USA believed that poor countries were more likely to turn to communism, so the Marshall Plan was designed. A fund to help countries that had suffered during the Second World War was set up. All European countries that agreed to the rules of free trade could apply. The USSR was unable to offer similar help, and so felt threatened as their economic weaknesses were exposed. |
| Given US perceptions that the USSR was trying to 'bolshevise' Europe, it is easy to understand how Stalin's defensive actions could be interpreted as aggressive and expansionist. For example, Stalin's claims on the Dardanelles reflected Soviet trade interests, but the USA saw this as ideologically driven expansion. |
| US policy assumed that communist ideology, and not national security, was the driving force behind USSR foreign policy. The US government ignored evidence, which showed that Soviet goals were limited and defensive and that global communism was not necessarily Soviet-backed. For example, the communists came to power in China (1949) with limited Soviet support and Stalin regarded Mao's regime as a rival rather than an ally. |
| The Truman Doctrine (1947) exaggerated the global communist threat in order to persuade Congress to support a policy of substantial aid to Greece and Turkey. Truman's position was based on the false assumption that the USSR was actively supporting the Greek communists in the civil war. |
| The US government mistakenly assumed that Stalin had deliberately engineered the Korean War. However, Truman knew nothing of the complex diplomacy between the Soviet leader, Kim Il-Sung and Mao, which preceded the conflict. Furthermore, the US administration may have given the North Korean, Chinese and Soviet regimes the false impression that the USA had written off Korea. |

## USSR – Misjudgements and misperceptions

| |
|---|
| Stalin's 1946 speech to the Supreme Soviet warned of a possible future war against capitalism in order to justify the introduction of further Five-Year Plans. The USA, however, interpreted this as a threat of war. Stalin's speech lacked clarity and his goals were often ambiguous. |
| The Marshall Plan was interpreted by the Kremlin as a calculated attempt to weaken Soviet security interests. The USSR responded with COMECON, which in turn was seen by the USA as a deliberate attempt to spread the Soviet economic model as part of world communism. |
| It could be argued that Stalin had been given Roosevelt and Churchill's unspoken approval for a defensive buffer zone at meetings before the end of the war (for example, at Teheran and Moscow). Stalin may therefore have felt that the USA was unfairly shifting its position, when it began to voice concerns over the future of post-war Europe. |
| American military superiority convinced Stalin that the USA would attack the USSR. Yet, in May 1945, the US government did not see the USSR as a likely threat. However, American reluctance to share nuclear technology only increased the Soviets' sense of vulnerability. Similarly, the first Soviet atomic detonation (1949) increased US fears and triggered a nuclear arms race. |
| From the 1930s onwards, Stalin showed growing signs of paranoia and became intensely suspicious. This meant that he was not necessarily able to assess post-war international events accurately. Many US decisions could be viewed as legitimate, for example, ending lend-lease once the war was over, and American unwillingness to see the German economy asset stripped in order to provide Soviet reparations. Stalin, however, interpreted these decisions as deliberate attempts to weaken the USSR. |

### Examiners' notes

Here you need to:
- understand the key features of the misjudgement and misperception interpretation of the development of the Cold War from 1945 to 1953 (make sure you can point to instances of misjudgement/misperception by both superpowers across the given timeframe)
- identify the strengths and weaknesses of this perspective; as this has become the dominant interpretation in recent years, it is important that you think about its shortcomings as an explanation for the development of the Cold War.

## The post-revisionist interpretation: an assessment

| | |
|---|---|
| **Strengths** | Identifies the important role played by superpower misjudgement, misperception and assumption in promoting Cold War tensions from 1945 |
| | Points out that the development of US–Soviet differences was due to the complex interaction of various factors |
| | Offers a more sophisticated and nuanced explanation of the development of the Cold War than the one-sided orthodox and revisionist explanations |
| **Weaknesses** | Post-revisionist explanations have been criticised for underestimating the importance of ideological motivation in US and Soviet actions |
| | As communist sources became available in the 1990s, the leading post-revisionist, John Lewis Gaddis, began to stress Stalin's role in creating the Cold War; thus, he appeared to move closer to the orthodox view |

## The Cold War and the USSR after Stalin

### The Death of Stalin, March 1953

By 1953, Stalin had imposed his system of control across the satellite states of Eastern Europe. This was part of consolidating Soviet domination, and consolidating the USSR's position in the Cold War. However, on the international stage, Stalin's final years were marked by a number of foreign policy failures, including the Berlin Blockade, the formation of NATO, and Yugoslavia's defection from the COMINFORM. Stalin's demise provided the new Soviet leadership with an opportunity to pursue more constructive domestic and foreign policies. It also raised the possibility of a new relationship between the superpowers and a relaxation of Cold War tensions.

### De-Stalinisation

Following Stalin's death, the Soviet *Politburo* endorsed the collective leadership of Georgi Malenkov, Vyacheslav Molotov, Nikolai Bulganin and Nikita Khrushchev to prevent another period of one-man rule. From 1953 to 1955, this collective leadership attempted to reform the Stalinist Soviet system by:

- ending 'personality cult' politics
- reforming the Secret Police (now renamed the KGB)
- arresting and executing Beria (1953), the feared head of the Secret Police (other Soviet leaders were worried that he wanted to be Stalin's hard-line successor)
- following a 'new course' in economic policy, which placed greater emphasis on the production of consumer goods.

### Khrushchev's Secret Speech, 1956

The Twentieth Party Congress (February 1956) witnessed the high point of de-Stalinisation. At a closed session of this gathering, Khrushchev denounced Stalin's reign of terror in a 'secret' speech which lasted for six hours. The deceased Soviet dictator was attacked for:

- promoting a cult of personality
- using purges and persecution to consolidate his personal rule
- reducing the Communist Party to a compliant body, which endorsed his absolute control.

Khrushchev's speech had a huge impact. In the USA, it was regarded as a sign that real change was taking place in the USSR. It also created the expectation of reform among the people of the Soviet satellite states in Eastern Europe. Evidently, de-Stalinisation had the potential to affect the USSR's foreign policy and was therefore significant for the development of the Cold War.

## Personality and politics: the role of Khrushchev in shaping superpower relations

During the years 1955 to 1958, Nikita Khrushchev was able to out-manoeuvre his chief rivals and emerge as the clear leader of the Soviet Union. From a peasant background with little formal education, Khrushchev was underestimated by political opponents (such as Malenkov, Beria and Molotov) who saw only an overweight rustic clown. In fact, he was intelligent, cunning and shrewd. He also contrasted sharply with the reclusive and sinister Stalin. Determined to present the 'human face of socialism', Khrushchev cultivated a 'man of the people' image and travelled widely to promote Soviet achievements. He even visited Britain (1956) and the USA (1959). Furthermore, his outgoing personality appeared to offer the prospect of improved US–Soviet relations.

According to the historian Geoffrey Roberts, Khrushchev's approach to the West was one of 'peaceful co-existence with a definite competitive edge'. The Soviet leader had been profoundly influenced by visits to the Russian front during the Second World War and was similarly appalled by the idea of nuclear attacks. For this reason, Khrushchev adopted a softer and more constructive tone than Stalin towards the West. This attitude was a crucial factor in making the summit diplomacy of the 1950s possible. He believed that the superpowers had to accept each other's existence and called for peaceful economic competition between socialism and capitalism.

At the same time, Khrushchev, as a committed communist, pursued competitive ideological and military policies in his dealings with the capitalist powers. Here, the more bombastic and unpredictable features of his personality surfaced. Equating national strength with nuclear capability, Khrushchev boasted falsely that the Soviet Union was producing missiles 'like sausages'. Such tactics were intended to convey the impression of Soviet superiority in military technology, when in fact, the USSR lagged behind. He was also prepared to undertake high-risk ventures (which led to the Berlin crisis of 1958–9 and the Cuban missile crisis of 1962) to test the USA's resolve and secure advantages for the USSR. At these points, Khrushchev, in John Lewis Gaddis's words, acted 'like a petulant child playing with a loaded gun'.

### Essential notes

Nikita Khrushchev (1894–1971), had previously held several senior party positions under Stalin. By 1958, he was the undisputed Soviet leader, having become both party head and prime minister. His foreign policy style – exuberant, bombastic and ideologically militant – reflected his personality. Khrushchev's removal from office in October 1964 was partly due to the humiliation of the Cuban missile crisis (1962).

### Essential notes

'Socialism with a human face' was a phrase used by Khrushchev to contrast his policies with the old policies of Stalin. The 'human face' that Khrushchev referred to included a greater emphasis on human comfort with more consumer goods and reduction in the scale of political terror.

### Essential notes

Khrushchev's approach to the Cold War was often contradictory. He believed in 'peaceful coexistence', yet he was often antagonistic. This can be explained by the fact that he never lost his faith in the superiority of communism and his desire to prove Soviet strength on the world stage. As a result, he was unwilling to back down when dealing with the USA, as this would be seen as a sign of weakness.

Georgi Malenkov

## Soviet motives for, and moves towards, peaceful co-existence

### Peaceful co-existence

Shortly after Stalin's death, Beria tried to forge a better relationship with the Western powers by proposing a reunified, neutral Germany. His initiative, however, was scuppered in June 1953 by Soviet repression of anti-communist demonstrations in East Germany. Two months later, the Soviet Prime Minister Georgi Malenkov called for a 'New Course' in foreign policy which focused on peaceful co-existence with the West. Malenkov was convinced that a capitalist–communist war was not inevitable. Consequently, the Soviet Union could devote more resources to raising living standards and developing consumer industries. Initially, Khrushchev opposed the New Course but once his rival Malenkov had been removed, he adopted effectively the same policy under the banner of 'Peaceful Co-existence'.

### Why did the Soviet Union pursue peaceful co-existence?

Stalin's death and the emergence of a more progressive Soviet leadership partly explain why the USSR adopted peaceful co-existence in the 1950s. Other important factors also encouraged both sides to follow more accommodating policies:

- As Marxists, the Soviet leadership believed in the inevitable triumph of communism over capitalism. Sooner or later, the West would be overwhelmed by an economic slump but until then the USSR could bide its time and avoid any damaging conflicts. Khrushchev summed up this position by saying 'Peaceful co-existence between different systems of government is possible but peaceful co-existence between different ideologies is not'.

- Khrushchev pursued peaceful co-existence, partly because he was confident that the USSR's economic output would soon overtake the West. In 1956 he claimed that, since 1929, Soviet industrial production had risen by 1.949 per cent but the corresponding figure for the USA was only 1.34 per cent. The Soviet leader also favoured this approach due to what he called 'the disintegration of the imperialist colonial system'. In his view, the newly decolonised states and national liberation movements would reject the imperialist Western states and look to the USSR for support.

- By the end of the 1940s both sides had consolidated their respective spheres of interest in Europe. Each also tacitly recognised the other's area of influence. This gave the superpowers a greater sense of security and made them more willing to negotiate.

- The economic and military implications of the nuclear arms race, which gathered pace in the 1950s, provided another reason for a more constructive USA–USSR relationship. The cost and sheer destructive power of these weapons had a sobering effect on the superpowers. As Khrushchev said, 'There are only two ways – either peaceful co-existence or the most destructive war in history. There is no third way'.

## Soviet peaceful co-existence – Key measures

| | |
|---|---|
| **End of the Korean War (July 1953)** | After Stalin's death, the new Soviet leadership (largely at Molotov and Malenkov's instigation) moved rapidly to bring the fighting in Korea to an end. This change of policy abandoned Stalin's hard-line approach in 1952 to continuing the conflict, and was influenced by Soviet concerns about the economic impact of prolonging the war. It represented a clear sign that the new USSR government wanted to manage its affairs in a different way from the Stalinist regime. As Malenkov stated at the time, 'there is no dispute or outstanding issue, which cannot be settled peacefully'. An Armistice was negotiated along the 38th parallel in July 1953 (see page 15). |
| **Cuts in the Red Army (from the mid-1950s)** | Khrushchev reduced Soviet conventional forces partly to convince the West of his peaceful intentions. In the second half of the 1950s, the size of the Red Army was decreased from 5.8 million to 3.7 million men. Further cuts (of 33 per cent) were announced in the early 1960s. It should be noted that Khrushchev scaled down the army for other reasons too. He wanted to save on military costs and was convinced that nuclear weapons afforded the USSR much better protection. |
| **The Austrian State Treaty (1955)** | Like Germany, Austria had been placed under joint occupation by the USA, the USSR, Britain and France in 1945. Subsequent four-power talks failed to settle Austria's future. The USSR extracted economic resources from their Austrian zone and the USA secretly rearmed the western Austrian sector and supported it with Marshall Aid. |
| | After overcoming Molotov's resistance in 1954, Khrushchev was ready to accept a neutral, rather than a permanently divided, Austria. He hoped this would be seen by the West as proof of his willingness to negotiate on key issues. The result was the Austrian State Treaty of 1955. This agreement, signed by the four occupying powers, removed all foreign troops and guaranteed Austria's independence as a neutral state. Furthermore, the treaty paved the way for the Geneva Summit (1955) and marked the first occasion since 1945 that Soviet troops had willingly left any part of Europe. |
| **Soviet withdrawal from Finland (1956)** | The Finnish–Soviet Peace Treaty (1947) formally ended the conflict between Russia and Finland which had taken place during the Second World War. Under its terms, Finland handed over border territory and $300 million in reparations to the USSR. The Soviet Union was also given a 50-year lease to the Porkkala peninsula, where it maintained a naval base. In 1955, Khrushchev, having once again surmounted Molotov's opposition, decided to remove the Soviet presence from Porkkala. The region was handed back to Finland in 1956. Khrushchev wanted this action to be seen in the West as further evidence that the USSR desired a more constructive relationship. Nevertheless, other considerations also prompted the Soviet withdrawal such as: Porkkala had little strategic value and Finland pledged to remain neutral and outside NATO. |
| **Other Soviet initiatives** | In 1953, the USSR settled border disputes with Turkey and Iran, re-established diplomatic relations with Greece, and formally recognised Israel. Two years later, the Soviet Union also recognised West Germany and restored relations with Tito's Yugoslavia. |

## Internal threats to the Soviet system: East Germany, Poland and Hungary

Between 1953 and 1956, popular expectations of change in the Eastern Bloc were encouraged by developments within, or policies pursued, by the USSR. These included:

- Khrushchev's rise and denunciation of Stalin
- his acceptance that there were 'many roads to socialism'
- better Soviet relations with the West and Yugoslavia.

The possibilities of change were limited due to the fact that the unity of the Eastern Bloc was crucial to the USSR's position in the Cold War. Any break between countries in the Eastern Bloc and the USSR would undermine Russia's prestige by implying that the people of Eastern Europe were unhappy with communism. The limits of this new mood of Soviet tolerance were to be severely tested during the 1950s, particularly in Poland and Hungary.

### Berlin Rising, June 1953

Following Stalin's death, the Soviet leadership adopted a new course in economic policy, placing greater emphasis on consumer goods. In East Germany, the hard-line Stalinist leader, Walter Ulbricht, continued to develop a strict command economy. In June 1953, he raised workers' production quotas without increasing pay, provoking demonstrations across East Germany. Some 400 000 workers took to the streets calling for free elections, a general strike and the lifting of quotas. The government responded with force, arresting and executing the protest leaders.

The Berlin Rising was significant for Cold War relations because it demonstrated the unpopularity of traditional communist policies and that their control over Eastern Europe was based on force rather than consent. It also indicated that the Soviet leadership were unwilling to allow greater independence in Eastern Europe. Nonetheless, while the USA made much of the Berlin Rising in anti-Soviet propaganda, the West was still unwilling to intervene in the Eastern Bloc for fear of provoking war.

### Poland 1956

The death of the Stalinist Polish communist leader, Boleslaw Beriut, in February 1956 sparked increasing calls for liberalisation in Poland. In June, large demonstrations in the industrial city of Poznan turned into anti-government protests. Discontent spread and there were strong calls for the Polish nationalist and moderate communist Wladyslaw Gomulka to be given power. In October, Khrushchev visited Warsaw to resolve the issue. Initially, Khrushchev tried to force Gomulka to back down, but once he realised the strength of feeling within the party and the country, he reluctantly relented. To stem the unrest, he agreed that Gomulka should become the party leader. Furthermore, some economic reforms were permitted on condition that Poland remained committed to the Warsaw Pact.

Reform in Poland was significant because it showed clear divisions in the communist world. Until 1953, the Cold War had been a struggle between communism in the East and the capitalist West. Events in Poland showed that there was a struggle going on within the communist camp. Khrushchev had been forced to compromise with the demands of the Polish communists. Moreover, Mao Zedong, leader of communist China, publically supported the Polish reformers. Clearly, Khrushchev's position within the communist world was weaker in 1956 than Stalin's had been in 1953, so his position in the Cold War was compromised.

### Hungary 1956

In July 1956, the anti-Stalinist communist, Imre Nagy, became premier of Hungary. However, Nagy's moderate policies failed to halt demands for reform. By late October protestors were calling for:

- multi-party democracy
- a free press
- Hungary's withdrawal from the Warsaw Pact.

To keep up with the popular mood, Nagy agreed to the three demands and declared Hungary a neutral country. The USSR viewed this as an act of open revolt; on 4 November, Red Army tanks entered Budapest to reassert Soviet control by force. By 11 November, the Soviet military had crushed the uprising and 'nationalist' Janos Kadar had replaced Nagy as premier. Kadar's new government reimposed centralised one-party control, arresting 35 000 protestors and executing 300 leaders of the uprising.

Hungary, like Poland, exposed the problems with Khrushchev's approach to the Eastern Bloc. Khrushchev encouraged limited reform, but this lead to demands that threatened to destroy the Eastern Bloc. This exposed the dictatorial nature of Soviet control. Hungary also exposed the weakness of the USA. Hungarian protestors had been encouraged by messages of support from Eisenhower and Dulles on 'Radio Free Europe', assuming that they would receive US military assistance. In fact, the West refused to stop the Red Army's brutal suppression of the rising. Political and military realities meant that the USA could not intervene to protect Hungary.

### Conclusion

The USSR responded differently to the 1956 Polish and Hungarian crises. In Poland the Communist Party stayed in control and Gomulka gave pledges of loyalty to the Soviet Union. In Hungary the Communist Party lost control of events and Nagy's decision to seek neutral status undermined the USSR's defensive barrier in Eastern Europe.

Soviet military action in Hungary demonstrated the USSR's determination to preserve its sphere of influence on its Western borders. After the Hungarian rising, the USSR concluded that the USA was unlikely to intervene in the 'Soviet' part of Europe.

### Essential notes

Wladyslaw Gomulka (1905–82), remained in Poland during the Second World War and became the Communist Party leader in 1945. He introduced economic reforms and abandoned collectivisation. Nevertheless, his popularity declined due to his:

- loyalty to the Warsaw Pact
- preservation of the one-party state
- accumulation of personal power.

Gomulka's failure to strengthen the economy generated popular unrest in 1970, which ended his political career.

### Essential notes

Imre Nagy (1896–1958), returned to Hungary at the end of the Second World War after a period of exile in the Soviet Union. As the Hungarian communist premier between 1953 and 1955, Nagy tried to introduce more liberal policies and economic reforms before being ousted in a power struggle. Due to popular pressure, he resumed the premiership in October 1956 but his support for radical reforms led to his overthrow by the Red Army the following month. He was arrested, taken to Romania and later executed.

## Eisenhower and Dulles, and the 'New Look' policy

### Eisenhower and Dulles take charge

Dwight Eisenhower's 1952 presidential victory appeared to signal the start of an uncompromising American approach to superpower relations. During the election campaign, Eisenhower had attacked Truman for being 'soft' on communism and rejected containment as 'futile and immoral'. Furthermore, prior to the election, John Foster Dulles had spoken about 'rolling back' communism and securing the 'liberation' of Eastern Europe from Soviet control. Indeed, once in office, Eisenhower and Dulles adopted the so-called 'New Look' policy, which emphasised hard-line Cold War diplomacy.

### The impact of the crushing of the 1956 Hungarian rising on the West

The Soviet suppression of the 1956 Hungarian revolt graphically revealed the limitations of Eisenhower's 'New Look' policy. Western reaction to the Red Army's brutal crushing of the rising was restricted to strong condemnation of the Soviet action, and America taking in 25 000 Hungarian refugees. There was growing scepticism about the USSR's new mood of 'accommodation', but political and military realities meant that the USA could not intervene to protect Hungary. Eastern Europe was a Soviet sphere of influence and the US government knew that any direct Western involvement in Hungary would almost certainly trigger a nuclear war with the USSR. Hungary revealed that, in practice, the USA could not 'roll back' communism in Eastern Europe. Containment remained the only possible American policy.

### Why did Eisenhower want better relations with the USSR?

In public, Eisenhower stressed his 'New Look' policy. However, in private, Eisenhower was prepared to act pragmatically to improve relations with the USSR. He did this for the following reasons:

- His military background made him strongly aware of the dangers of a nuclear conflict that could 'destroy civilisation'.

- Eisenhower was concerned that military spending (12% of GNP in the mid-1950s) was too high and that it threatened to impinge on US living standards. Better relations with the USSR would decrease the likelihood of nuclear war and therefore the government could reduce military spending.

- Intelligence gathered by U-2 spy planes showed that the USSR was considerably behind in the arms race. Therefore, Eisenhower knew that USSR could not win a nuclear war. This gave the USA the upper hand in negotiations between the superpowers.

The 'New Look' policy went hand in hand with better relations with the USSR because, by strengthening the USA's position, Eisenhower hoped to force the USSR to negotiate rather than risk war.

| Key features of Eisenhower's 'New Look' policy on the Cold War |
| --- |
| **Massive retaliation** |
| In January 1954, Dulles announced a policy of 'massive retaliatory power', that the USA would make greater use of nuclear threats and place less reliance on conventional weapons.<br><br>The circumstances under which the USA would unleash 'massive retaliation' were kept deliberately vague to put opponents at a disadvantage. |
| **Brinkmanship** |
| Massive retaliation formed part of Dulles' wider policy of 'brinkmanship'.<br><br>Instances of US brinkmanship in the 1950s were:<br><br>• In 1953 the US warned China that if the Korean War was not brought to a speedy conclusion it would use nuclear weapons. An Armistice was signed shortly afterwards.<br><br>• When Chinese communists shelled the nationalist-held islands of Quemoy and Matsu in 1954–5, the US once again issued nuclear threats. Mao's forces stopped their military action. |
| **Increased use of covert operations** |
| From 1953, the US government made regular use of covert operations. Examples of this, in practice, include:<br><br>• The 1953 CIA operation to ensure that the pro-western Iranian Muhammad Reza Pahlavi was installed as the Shah of Iran. The success of this operation gave America an ally on the USSR's border.<br><br>• The 1954 CIA-backed coup against the left-wing Guatemalan President, Jacobo Arbenz Guzman.<br><br>• The development of U-2 spy planes to aid intelligence gathering. |
| **Domino Theory (1954)** |
| US policy was also influenced by Eisenhower's domino theory (April 1954). The theory maintained that if Vietnam succumbed to communism, it would be followed in turn by Laos, Cambodia, Thailand, Malaya, Indonesia and the Philippines. These concerns prompted the formation of SEATO (the South-East Asian Treaty Organisation) in September 1954, a military alliance between the USA and the countries of South East Asia. |
| **Eisenhower Doctrine (1957)** |
| The Eisenhower Doctrine was designed to halt communist penetration of the Middle East and to stop the Middle East's oil supplies from falling into hostile hands. It committed US economic and military support to protect the independence of any state in the region, which was threatened by armed communist aggression. |

## Essential notes

SEATO was formed in 1954. This alliance of western powers (USA, Britain, France, Australia and New Zealand) and their allies (Pakistan, the Philippines and Thailand) attempted to prevent the spread of communism in South-East Asia. SEATO had only a limited impact in the region and its establishment angered China.

## Examiners' notes

In order to do well in the exam it is important to show that you understand the significance of the events that you describe. For example, as well as being able to describe Khrushchev's policy of peaceful co-existence you should also be able to explain how it affected the relationship between the superpowers in the Cold War. Equally, as well being able to describe the Hungarian uprising, you should be able to explain how it impacted on Cold War relations. You could do this by analysing the implications of the uprising for Soviet control over the Eastern Bloc and by analysing the reasons for the USA's refusal to send military assistance.

Map of Geneva settlement of the Indochina War

## Essential notes

FDR stands for Federal Republic of Germany (West Germany) and GDR is the German Democratic Republic (East Germany).

## The 'Geneva spirit' and conference diplomacy, 1954–61

Stalin's death and the end of the Korean War led a renewal of superpower conference diplomacy between 1954 and 1961. This process was assisted by Khrushchev's pursuit of peaceful co-existence and Eisenhower's belief in the benefits of face-to-face meetings to address problems. Overall, these negotiations improved US–Soviet relations, but failed to tackle important issues such as the future of Germany and the arms race.

### Geneva Conference, April–July 1954

The Geneva Conference was the first indication of the success of superpower diplomacy. USA, USSR, Britain and France met at Geneva to discuss Korea and Indochina. No progress was made on a Korean peace treaty, but a settlement was negotiated about the Indochina War (1946–54; see Essential notes opposite). Under this agreement, which the US refused to sign but pledged not to undermine:

- A ceasefire was declared and French troops were to be withdrawn.

- Laos and Cambodia were established as independent states.

- Vietnam was temporarily divided into a communist north (under Ho Chi Minh and the Viet-Minh) and Bao Dai's regime in the south.

- The country was to be reunited through free elections by 1956.

However, Ngo Din Diem, who replaced Bao Dai as the leader of South Vietnam in 1955, cancelled the scheduled elections. Polls had predicted that Ho Chi Minh would win. During 1958–9 communist guerrillas, supported by North Vietnam, began a military campaign against Diem's unpopular and corrupt government. In 1960, these anti-Diem forces became the National Liberation Front (the so-called 'Vietcong'). Eisenhower provided large-scale economic aid to South Vietnam in its struggle against the communist North.

### Geneva Summit, July 1955

The Geneva Summit was the first East–West Summit of the Cold War. It involved 'the Big Four': the leaders of Britain and France as well as the two superpowers. The meeting helped to shape superpower relations by establishing a good working relationship between the leaders of the two superpowers, and by restarting face-to-face diplomacy between the leaders of the USSR and the USA, which had ceased after the Potsdam Conference of 1945.

However, agreement could not be reached on the following issues:

- **Germany** – Soviet proposals to neutralise Germany were rejected by the West because of concerns that this would increase Soviet influence in central Europe and undermine the FDR's pro-western stance. The West also refused Soviet requests to recognise East Germany. On the issue of German reunification, the West pressed for free elections but the USSR wanted negotiations between the GDR and the FDR. The Soviets feared that a united Germany would join the Western alliance against the USSR.

- **European security arrangements** – Soviet plans were put forward for replacing NATO and the Warsaw Pact with a collective security system. The West viewed this as a communist scheme to dismantle NATO.

- **'Open skies' initiative** – Eisenhower suggested that, in order to prevent surprise attacks and verify arms agreements, both superpowers should be allowed to take aerial photographs over the other's airspace. Khrushchev rejected this 'open skies' proposal as an espionage plot.

In spite of the disagreements, the Geneva Summit created a changed mood in the tone of superpower relations. The Soviet newspaper *Pravda* spoke of the 'Geneva spirit' and hinted at a thaw in superpower relations.

## Khrushchev's US visit and the Camp David Summit, September 1959

Camp David was significant as it was the first summit involving only the USA and the USSR. Equally, it took place following the death of the stridently anti-communist Dulles, a fact that led Khrushchev to conclude that a deal between the superpowers might, at last, be possible. Eisenhower too hoped for agreement before he left office as President.

The meeting built on the relationship established at Geneva. Indeed, the two leaders agreed to hold a full summit in 1960 and resolved to settle disputes peacefully. However, the leaders were unable to reach an agreement on important matters such as Germany and disarmament.

## Paris Summit, May 1960

The Paris Summit was less successful due to Khrushchev and Eisenhower adopting a harder line. In the West, the French and West German governments, were fearful that the US would give ground to the Soviet Union on key issues such as Germany. At the same time, Khrushchev was under pressure from China who accused him of adopting 'soft' policies towards the West. As a result, neither side appeared particularly keen to negotiate but it was the U-2 spy plane incident of May 1960 (see page 40) that led to the rapid collapse of the summit.

## Vienna Summit, June 1961

The Vienna Summit marked a new stage in superpower relations. Kennedy had recently been elected as US's President and Khrushchev attempted to capitalise on Kennedy's inexperience, and his recent humiliation over the Bay of Pigs fiasco, by adopting an aggressive stance:

- The Soviet Union would continue to support 'wars of national liberation' because of the dominance of colonial and capitalist powers.

- The West should recognise the sovereign status of East Germany.

- The Berlin question should be settled on Soviet terms within six months.

The only constructive result of the summit was an agreement to ensure a neutral and independent Laos. Kennedy was shaken by Khrushchev's behaviour but did not back down. Ultimately, the head of the USSR misjudged Kennedy as weak – a mistake that would be revealed clearly during the Cuban missile crisis of 1962.

### Essential notes

Indochina War, 1946–54

Indochina (the region now containing Vietnam, Laos and Cambodia) had been a French colony since the 1860s. In 1946, French negotiations with the nationalist Viet-Minh movement in Vietnam broke down. By then, the Viet-Minh, led by the communist Ho Chi Minh, had established a stronghold in North Vietnam. The failure of the talks led to a brutal colonial guerrilla war. In 1949, Bao Dai, the former emperor of Vietnam, was installed by the French as the head of a pro-Western Vietnamese government. Eventually, the Viet-Minh's guerrilla tactics undermined French resources and resolve. When the Viet-Minh defeated the French garrison at Dien Bien Phu (1954), the French government decided to withdraw from Indochina. The Geneva conference followed shortly afterwards.

## Examiners' notes

You will need to understand the impact of the U-2 incident of 1960 and the reasons for continuing superpower tensions over Berlin between 1958 and 1961.

## Essential notes

The Lockheed U-2 spy plane was developed by the CIA and deployed from 1956. It flew at a height of 22 900 metres (75 000 feet) and had a range of 3200 kilometres (2000 miles). Equipped with cameras and electronic equipment, the U-2 could monitor radio transmissions and take high-resolution reconnaissance photographs.

## End of the thaw: the U-2 incident and the impact of the Berlin crisis

Although the post-Stalin thaw had eased superpower tension, the era of peaceful co-existence began to unravel from the late 1950s. Two important developments, which helped to harden US–Soviet relations during this period, were the U-2 incident and East–West disagreements over the German Question.

### The U-2 incident, 1960

On 1 May 1960, a US U-2 spy plane was shot down by a Soviet missile over Russia. The pilot, Gary Powers, was captured. Initially, the US claimed that that spy flights over Russia had never taken place and that the downed aircraft was a weather research plane that had strayed off course. Khrushchev exposed this cover story by displaying the U-2's espionage equipment. The Soviet leader also demanded a US apology for spying and lying. Eventually, on 11 May, Eisenhower admitted the truth and announced U-2 flights would end but refused to apologise. The Paris Summit convened three days later. Unable to secure a US public apology, Khrushchev stormed out of the meeting and cancelled Eisenhower's planned visit to Russia. In 1962 Powers was exchanged for Rudolf Abel, a New York-based Soviet spy. The U-2 incident boosted Khrushchev's standing and made him more determined to exert Soviet influence. His confrontational approach was partly due to the deteriorating Sino-Soviet relationship. Mao strongly opposed peaceful co-existence with the West and so Khrushchev's tough stance on the U-2 issue was probably designed to reassure the Chinese leader.

### The German Question, 1958–61

When West Germany joined NATO in 1955, the USSR feared that a rearmed FRG would press for reunification. The Soviet Union responded by creating the Warsaw Pact. Although West Germany and the USSR established diplomatic links, relations were hampered by the Hallstein Doctrine of 1955 which maintained that West Germany would regard diplomatic recognition of the GDR as an unfriendly act, as it implied acceptance of the division of the country.

West Berlin posed the USSR several problems since it was a capitalist enclave in a communist state, an escape route to the West (between 1951 and 1961 over four million defected from East Germany via West Berlin), a major source of Western intelligence about the Soviet Bloc, and a centre for pro-US radio propaganda transmitted across Eastern Europe.

By the late 1950s Khrushchev faced increasing pressure concerning the German Question. In September 1958 the Western powers rejected East German–West German talks, and the Soviet leader was being pressed by the East German regime to guarantee the GDR's security since the West refused to recognise East Germany, and take measures to halt the mass defections to the West.

## The Second Berlin Crisis, 1958–9

In November 1958, Khrushchev attempted to impose a Soviet solution to the German problem:

- West Berlin should become a demilitarised 'free city'.

- East–West talks on a German peace treaty should commence.

- Access routes to Berlin would be handed over to East Germany in six months (to force the West to deal directly with East Germany).

The USA, Britain and France rejected Khrushchev's demands and Dulles stated that NATO would retaliate if Western access to Berlin was denied. Khrushchev backed down and a foreign ministers' conference in Geneva (1960) temporarily eased tensions over Germany.

## The Third Crisis, Berlin Wall, August 1961

When Khrushchev and Kennedy met in Vienna (June 1961), the Soviet leader insisted that the West should recognise East Germany and that the US should withdraw from Berlin by the end of that year.

Kennedy rejected these demands, arguing that Berlin was central to US security interests. On 25 July, the President publicly pledged that the US would not be driven out of Berlin and announced increases in the armed forces. Khrushchev did not want a war over Berlin but could not allow the exodus of East Germans to continue. In August 1961, Khrushchev surprised the West by building a wall, which would prevent free movement between East and West Berlin. In response to the Berlin Wall, Kennedy considered a limited nuclear first strike against the USSR, but this option was dropped once it became clear there was no direct threat to West Berlin. Khrushchev's action stemmed the flood of defectors to the West and the USA accepted the division of Berlin (see the map). The Berlin Wall symbolised East–West hostility and became the enduring image of the Cold War.

## The Fourth Berlin Crisis, October 1961

After the Berlin Wall crisis, Kennedy sent General Lucius Clay to Berlin as his representative. Clay's aim was to resist Soviet and East German pressure. In October 1961, a US diplomat could not enter East Berlin as he refused to show his passport. This contravened an agreement allowing free passage without passports for Western and Soviet personnel. Clay responded by providing a US military patrol to escort the diplomat into East Berlin. Armed US soldiers accompanied US citizens. US tanks were also stationed at Checkpoint Charlie, the chief crossing point between East and West Berlin. On 27 October, 33 Soviet tanks entered East Berlin; 23 were positioned at the Brandenburg Gate and 10 stopped at Checkpoint Charlie, facing the US tanks. This tense stand-off ensured that the US garrison in Berlin, NATO and Strategic Air Command were put on alert. Khrushchev authorised the Soviet commander in Berlin to return fire if attacked. Kennedy contacted Khrushchev directly and proposed a joint staged removal of these forces. This solution broke the deadlock. After 16 hours 'nose to nose', the tanks on both sides withdrew, one by one.

Berlin Wall
West Berlin
East Berlin
East Germany

## Examiners' notes

Why did the Cold War continue? There were several reasons why the era of peaceful co-existence failed to end the Cold War. These included the following:

- US–Soviet ideological hostility continued (for example, Khrushchev rejected the notion of ideological peaceful co-existence).

- The accelerating arms race, conducted in secret, promoted fear and suspicion on both sides.

- Decolonisation and the 'end of empire' opened up new areas for superpower competition and conflict (such as the Middle East and South-East Asia).

- China's criticism of peaceful co-existence put pressure on Khrushchev to adopt a harder line with the West (for example, the Paris Summit and the U-2 incident).

- US–Soviet failure to resolve specific divisive (disruptive) issues such as the future of Germany.

## Essential notes

America's nuclear monopoly ended on 28 August 1949 when the Soviet Union successfully tested a plutonium bomb (code-named First Lightning), at Semipalatinsk-21 in north-east Kazakhstan.

## Essential notes

Nuclear fusion, or hydrogen bombs, were based on the fusion of the nuclei of hydrogen isotopes. This process releases huge amounts of energy and radiation.

Nuclear fusion bombs were also known as thermonuclear weapons because fusion took place at extremely high temperatures.

## Development of weapons technology and advanced delivery systems

### 1949: Russia acquires the atomic bomb

The emerging Cold War led to a superpower arms race, driven by nuclear technology, which became part of the wider ideological competition to demonstrate the 'superiority' of US capitalism or Soviet communism.

In 1949 the USA, having the only bomb, had a nuclear monopoly and the CIA concluded that the USSR would not develop an atomic bomb before mid-1953. Yet, a Soviet nuclear test occurred in 1949. This event led to the start of the thermonuclear arms race and superpower rivalry.

### The thermonuclear arms race begins

In January 1950, President Truman announced that the USA would build a 'super' bomb, or hydrogen bomb. This weapon would be based on nuclear fusion, but would deliver an explosive force three to five times greater than that produced by nuclear fission. The decision was prompted by:

- the speed with which the USSR had ended the USA's nuclear monopoly
- the Berlin Blockade of 1948–9
- the establishment of the People's Republic of China in October 1949
- the discovery of a Soviet nuclear spy ring
- the assumption that the USSR would build such a weapon anyway.

The successful testing of a US hydrogen bomb, code-named Ivy Mike, on a Pacific island in November 1952, led to a thermonuclear arms race. These weapons were massively more powerful than the atomic bombs dropped on Japan.

'Little Boy' (USA) dropped on Hiroshima, August 1945 13 kilotons

'Ivy Mike' (USA) Nov. 1952 10 megatons

'Joe 4' (USSR) Aug. 1953 400 kilotons

'Castle Bravo' (USA) Mar. 1954 15 megatons

RDS-37 (USSR) Nov. 1955 1.6 megatons

'Tsar Bomba' (USSR) Oct. 1961 50 megatons

Key thermonuclear tests 1952–61

### Delivering the bomb by plane

Initially, both the USA and the Soviet Union developed reliable aircraft to carry the thermonuclear bomb to its target. From 1953, 40 per cent of US defence funds were allocated to the air force; by 1955, the USA owned the B52 Stratofortress, the first bomber with intercontinental range.

Furthermore, under the control of General Curtis 'Bombs Away' LeMay, Strategic Air Command (SAC) became the USA's main nuclear strike force, with bombers placed on 24-hour alert. The Soviets could not compete with SAC but responded in 1956 with the TU20 Bear, copied from the B52 design. However, the drawbacks to delivering the bomb by plane were that bombers were relatively slow and could be shot down, and the USSR had no access to airbases near US territory.

## The development of rocket technology

From the early 1950s, both superpowers were also developing rocket-based nuclear weapon delivery systems. In May 1957, the Soviet Union successfully tested the world's first intercontinental ballistic missile (ICBM), capable of carrying a thermonuclear warhead. Five months later, the USSR launched *Sputnik*, the first space satellite, and, in November 1957, put *Sputnik II* into orbit with a dog named Laika as its passenger. By 1959, the Soviet Strategic Rocket Force was a new section of the Soviet military. The USSR's lead in rocket technology was confirmed in April 1961 when Yuri Gagarin (in *Vostok I*) became the first man in space.

## The 'missile gap' 1957–61

The USSR's successes with the ICBM, *Sputnik* and *Vostok I* projects led to US fears that the Soviets had more advanced military technology. The findings of the CIA Gaither Report of November 1957 and the failure of the first US Vanguard satellite launch reinforced the idea of a 'missile gap' in the Soviet Union's favour. However, the USSR's achievements were less impressive than they appeared. Khrushchev devoted a lot of attention to impressive demonstrations of Soviet power. 'Tsar Bomba', for example, showed that the USSR could create a powerful nuclear bomb – but could not mass-produce these bombs. Even though the USSR was often first to achieve a technological success, the USA was never far behind:

- The USA possessed more nuclear weapons than the USSR and launched its own satellite, *Explorer*, in January 1958. The USA also developed its own ICBMs, culminating in the *Minuteman*, which was far superior to Soviet missiles.

- Government intelligence gathered by US U-2 spy-planes and (in 1960–61) the CIA satellite *Discoverer* revealed that the USSR had relatively few bombers and operational missiles.

- The USA also deployed intermediate range ballistic missiles (IRBMs) in Britain, Italy and Turkey.

- In 1958, Eisenhower increased funding for science education and research to maintain the USA's lead, and in July 1960, the USA deployed *Polaris*, the world's first submarine-launched ballistic missile (SLBM), which was also more advanced than similar Soviet weapons.

By the early 1960s a 'balance of terror' existed between the two superpowers. The arms race had reached the point of mutually assured destruction (MAD) (see page 45).

### Essential notes

The success of the Soviet *Sputnik* project prompted the USA to establish the National Aeronautics and Space Administration (NASA) in 1958. NASA's director reported directly to the President.

### Essential notes

| Strategic bombers | | | |
|---|---|---|---|
| | 1956 | 1960 | 1965 |
| USA | 560 | 550 | 630 |
| USSR | 60 | 175 | 200 |

### Essential notes

| Number of US atomic bombs | | |
|---|---|---|
| 1950 | 1955 | 1962 |
| 288 | 2422 | 27100 |

| ICBMs | | | |
|---|---|---|---|
| | 1960 | 1962 | 1964 |
| USA | 20 | 295 | 835 |
| USSR | 30 | 75 | 200 |

| SLBMs | | |
|---|---|---|
| | 1962 | 1965 |
| USA | 145 | 500 |
| USSR | 45 | 125 |

### Essential notes

According to the Gaither Report on deterrence and survival (which was leaked to the press), the USSR held a missile lead, a three-to-one Soviet–US 'missile gap' would develop and the US needed a $44 billion defence budget over five years to close the gap and build civilian fallout shelters.

## Examiners' notes

You need to know what impact the arms race had on the nature of the Cold War from 1949 to 1963. Here, focus on:

- superpower military strategy in the early nuclear age
- the stabilising and destabilising effects of the arms race on the Cold War.

## Essential notes

The doctrine of nuclear deterrence was first put forward in the mid-1940s. It maintained that:

- in the nuclear age military victory in total war was not possible
- a country's ability to launch a retaliatory nuclear strike should survive an enemy's initial attack
- this ability would discourage enemy use of nuclear weapons.

Limited war is a war that is fought with conventional weapons, is limited in scale, and is restricted to a particular area or region.

## Essential notes

Massive retaliation was a nuclear doctrine, which:

- emphasised retaliation by any means against threats to US vital interests
- was deliberately vague about the exact circumstances that would trigger a US nuclear response.

## 'Balance of terror'

Winston Churchill remarked that nuclear weapons had created a post-war 'balance of terror'. Indeed, the awesome destructive capacity of the superpowers' nuclear arsenals played a major role in shaping US and Soviet conduct in the Cold War from 1949 until 1963. The obvious danger of nuclear war prevented the USA and the USSR from engaging in direct armed conflict, and ultimately forced them to co-operate at key points (such as the Cuban missile crisis).

### Nuclear deterrence and limited war

The USSR's acquisition of the atomic bomb and the Soviets' determination to match US developments in this type of weaponry made nuclear deterrence a strategic reality for both sides. Deterrence was linked to the concept of limited war, which first emerged during the Korean War (1950–1953). To avoid the dangers of superpower nuclear escalation in the Korean conflict, the following steps were taken for nuclear deterrence:

- Stalin did not intervene directly in the war.
- Truman refused to use nuclear weapons against China.
- The US restricted the combat zone to Korea.

### Massive retaliation

US confidence about its nuclear superiority in the 1950s (when it held at least a 10 to 1 advantage in nuclear weapons over the Soviet Union) led the Eisenhower administration to introduce the doctrine of massive retaliation (1954). This strategy of greater reliance on nuclear weapons involved the use of brinkmanship (going to the brink of nuclear war) to force an enemy to back down. The strategy was also partly designed to reduce conventional arms spending. Similar policies were adopted by the USSR (1955) and Britain (1957). Critics argued: massive retaliation was unrealistic; the USA would only use nuclear weapons in an emergency.

### Flexible response and counterforce

President Kennedy and his Defence Secretary, Robert McNamara, rejected massive retaliation as being too rigid. Instead, they favoured a flexible response strategy, which considered the possibility of a limited nuclear war. As part of this new approach, McNamara developed a 'second strike' capability (based on bombers, ICBMs and submarines) so the USA could strike back at Russia after suffering a nuclear attack. In 1962, he also introduced the counterforce strategy to make the USSR's military installations, rather than Soviet cities, the main targets of any future US nuclear strike. The USSR did not endorse flexible response tactics and based its plans on an all-out nuclear attack.

Flexible response was hugely expensive and raised basic questions about how a nuclear war could be 'limited' or 'managed'. When faced with the October 1962 crisis, for example, Kennedy threatened 'a full retaliatory response upon the Soviet Union' if any Western nation was hit by Cuban missiles. A further difficulty with flexible response was the USA's inability to target Soviet nuclear sites accurately.

## Mutual assured destruction (MAD)

The failings of flexible response and the gradual erosion of US nuclear superiority from the early 1960s led to another shift in American nuclear strategy. In 1963 McNamara began to emphasise nuclear deterrence and talk of the USSR's 'assured destruction' in any conflict. By the mid-late 1960s, however, when the Soviet Union had achieved basic nuclear parity with the USA, the superpowers had reached the position of mutual assured destruction or mutual deterrence. The Soviets never used the term 'nuclear deterrence' but it also underpinned their strategy.

## The impact of the arms race on the Cold War

### Stabilising effects

- The deterrent effect of nuclear weapons prevented direct US–Soviet confrontation.

- The presence of nuclear weapons meant that the superpowers respected each other's sphere of influence and did not intervene, for example, in Hungary (1956).

- The superpowers had to co-operate to regulate the nuclear threat, such as the removal of nuclear missiles from Cuba and Turkey (1962–1963), Nuclear Test Ban Treaty (1963), Washington–Moscow 'hotline' (1963).

- The US and Soviet leaders were aware of living in the nuclear age and acting responsibly, for example, Khrushchev withdrew the offer of help in the nuclear programme from Chinese communist leader Mao Zedong.

### Destabilising effects

- Soviet acquisition of the atomic bomb (1949) precipitated a spiralling arms race. Both sides competed to develop more and more powerful and sophisticated weapons such as the hydrogen bomb (1952), ICBMs (1957) and SLBMs (1960).

- The culture of secrecy surrounding the development of nuclear weapons led to superpower fears that the other side had military superiority: the impact of the Gaither Report (1957) (page 43).

- Nuclear weapons encouraged superpower brinkmanship, which could have resulted in total devastation, for example, the US doctrine of 'massive retaliation' (1954) and the Cuban missile crisis (1962).

- The cost of nuclear weapons imposed huge financial strains on both sides. This had a destabilising effect on superpower relations in two ways: Khrushchev compensated for the USSR's relative weakness by adopting an antagonistic approach to negotiations with the West, and his decision to station Soviet nuclear weapons in Cuba was due to the fact that basing short-range missiles in Cuba was cheaper than basing long-range weapons in the USSR.

- Nuclear weapons did not stop other forms of superpower competition for influence in the 1950s and early 1960s. For example, Soviet economic and military aid to developing countries such as Egypt; US support for anti-communist regimes in South Vietnam, South Korea and Taiwan.

### Essential notes

Flexible response was a policy that stressed a range of military options such as:

- using smaller nuclear missiles to achieve limited objectives in a war without escalating to a full nuclear exchange.
- building up conventional armed forces to deal with wars of 'national liberation' in the Third World.

### Essential notes

Mutual assured destruction (MAD) is based on the understanding that neither superpower could defeat the other in a nuclear war without also being destroyed.

## Essential notes

Fidel Castro (1926–) was born into a middle-class Cuban family and took a law degree at the University of Havana. After ousting Batista in 1959, he became increasingly reliant on the USSR and declared Cuba a socialist state. Castro later assisted other radical groups in Latin America. During the 1970s, Castro also sent Cuban military forces to help Marxist governments in Angola and Ethiopia.

## The causes of the Cuban missile crisis, 1962

### The Cuban Revolution, 1959

Since the end of Spanish rule in 1898, Cuba was under the political and economic influence of the USA. By the mid-20th century, the USA owned much of the Cuban economy (such as industry, railways, telephone system, and electricity and sugar production). From 1933, Cuba was ruled by Fulgencio Batista, a ruthless military dictator. He encouraged economic involvement of the USA in return for US support for his brutal, corrupt and unpopular regime. In January 1959, Batista was overthrown by revolutionaries, led by Fidel Castro. Batista fled into exile.

### Growing US–Cuban tension, 1959–61

Initially, Castro seemed to be a liberal nationalist and had no programme to nationalise US interests in Cuba. However, relations between Cuba and the USA soon deteriorated, and Castro became increasingly dependent on the Soviet Union. Tensions between Cuba and the USA increased:

- Castro's meeting with US Vice-President Richard Nixon in New York (April 1959) did not go well. Nixon concluded that Castro was a communist.

- Castro's imprisonment and execution of some of Batista's supporters was condemned in the USA.

- Many Batista supporters fled to the USA where they campaigned for a US-backed invasion of Cuba. This hardened Castro's attitude.

- Castro wanted to make Cuba independent of US influence, so he distributed land to poor peasants who had previously been exploited by Batista and US business interests.

- US-owned oil companies in Cuba refused to refine the cheaper Soviet oil. Castro responded by nationalising the refineries (the USA refused Cuba's compensation offer).

- In February 1960, Castro signed a trade deal with the Soviet Union to nationalise US interests in Cuba that were worth over $1 billion.

- In July 1960, the USA imposed an economic blockade on Cuba, thereby refusing to buy its sugar (the island's chief export). The Soviet Union bought the crop, and sent Castro petrol after the USA refused to ship supplies.

- In early 1961 Castro formally embraced communism.

## The Bay of Pigs Invasion, April 1961

In 1961, President Kennedy authorised a CIA-backed invasion of Cuba. The aim was to spark a popular revolt on the island to overthrow Castro. Some 1400 lightly armed anti-Castro Cuban exiles landed at the Bay of Pigs, but were quickly overwhelmed by the Cuban army and air force. This failed assault was a deep humiliation for Kennedy, who could not conceal the USA's involvement. Castro reacted by entering into a defensive agreement with the USSR, which brought Soviet weapons and military advisers to Cuba. By early 1962, Khrushchev had supplied the island with MiG jets and surface-to-air missiles (SAMs).

## Operation Mongoose, October 1961

Six months after the Bay of Pigs fiasco, the CIA (with Kennedy's full support) launched Operation Mongoose, a secret programme designed to destabilise the Cuban regime and topple Castro. Between January and July 1962, some 60 000 acts of sabotage, ranging from murder to arson, were carried out on the island as part of this operation. The USA also held large-scale military exercises in the Caribbean to increase the pressure on Cuba and demonstrate American armed might. Both Castro and the USSR expected the USA to invade.

## Soviet nuclear weapons on Cuba, 1962

In early September 1962 the USSR secretly started to install 24 SS-4 medium range ballistic missile launchers in Cuba, and 16 longer-range SS-5 missile launchers. Each launcher would hold two missiles, both containing a one megaton nuclear warhead. The Soviets also sent 42 jet bombers, 42 jet fighters, 24 advanced SAMs, four elite army regiments, two tank battalions and over 40 000 troops and other personnel. Khrushchev described this military build-up as 'throwing a hedgehog at Uncle Sam's underpants'. His precise motives for undertaking such a risky venture are not entirely clear but probably included the following:

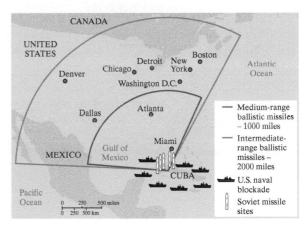

Map of Cuba and the USA, showing the missile bases and ranges to key US cities

- to defend Cuba from an expected US invasion

- to bargain for the removal of US nuclear missiles from Turkey and Italy

- to further humiliate Kennedy after the Bay of Pigs failure

- to put pressure on the West to leave Berlin

- to achieve nuclear parity with the USA by making US cities more vulnerable to attack.

## Examiners' notes

You need to understand how the actual crisis developed and was resolved in October 1962. Consider how Khrushchev and Kennedy's actions made the crisis more acute and paved the way for a solution.

## The Cuban missile crisis, October 1962

### The world on the brink

On 14 October 1962, a US U-2 spy plane photographed Soviet nuclear missile sites near San Cristobal in western Cuba. The ensuing crisis, which lasted until 28 October, was the most serious incident of the Cold War and took the superpowers to the brink of nuclear conflict.

### What influenced the USA's actions during the Cuban missile crisis?

The diagram shows what influenced the USA's actions during the Cuban missile crisis:

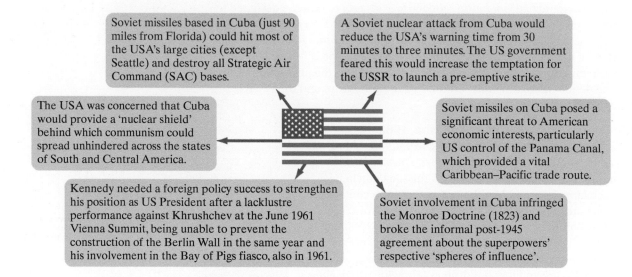

Soviet missiles based in Cuba (just 90 miles from Florida) could hit most of the USA's large cities (except Seattle) and destroy all Strategic Air Command (SAC) bases.

A Soviet nuclear attack from Cuba would reduce the USA's warning time from 30 minutes to three minutes. The US government feared this would increase the temptation for the USSR to launch a pre-emptive strike.

The USA was concerned that Cuba would provide a 'nuclear shield' behind which communism could spread unhindered across the states of South and Central America.

Soviet missiles on Cuba posed a significant threat to American economic interests, particularly US control of the Panama Canal, which provided a vital Caribbean–Pacific trade route.

Kennedy needed a foreign policy success to strengthen his position as US President after a lacklustre performance against Khrushchev at the June 1961 Vienna Summit, being unable to prevent the construction of the Berlin Wall in the same year and his involvement in the Bay of Pigs fiasco, also in 1961.

Soviet involvement in Cuba infringed the Monroe Doctrine (1823) and broke the informal post-1945 agreement about the superpowers' respective 'spheres of influence'.

## Essential notes

The Monroe Doctrine was a policy that was announced by the early 19th Century US President James Monroe. It stated that the USA would regard any attempt by a European power to colonise the 'American continents' as an 'unfriendly' act.

| Cuba: America's war of words |
| --- |
| 'It shall be the policy of this nation to regard any nuclear missile launched from Cuba against any nation in the Western hemisphere as an attack by the Soviet Union on the United States, requiring a full retaliatory response upon the Soviet Union ... I call upon Chairman Khrushchev to halt this clandestine, reckless and provocative threat to world peace ... He has an opportunity now to move the world back from the abyss of destruction'. |
| President Kennedy, US TV address, 22 October 1962 |
| 'Well, let me say something to you, Mr Ambassador. We do have evidence ... it is clear and uncontrovertible ... Do you, Ambassador Zorin, deny that the USSR has placed and is placing missile sites in Cuba? Yes or no?' |
| US Ambassador Adlai Stevenson challenges Soviet Ambassador Valerian Zorin at the UN, 25 October 1962 |

## The crisis, day by day, in October 1962

| Sunday 14 October | Monday 15 October | Tuesday 16 October | Wednesday 17 October |
|---|---|---|---|
| A US U-2 spy plane photographs nuclear missile launch sites in Cuba. | US National Photographic Intelligence Centre reviews and verifies the U-2 pictures. | President Kennedy assembles an Executive Committee of the National Security Council (ExComm) to discuss US military and diplomatic response. | During the ExComm meeting, the Joint Chiefs of Staff press for an air strike. Another U-2 flight reveals IRBMs (SS-5 missiles) on Cuba. |
| **Thursday 18 October** | **Friday 19 October** | **Saturday 20 October** | **Sunday 21 October** |
| Kennedy meets Andrei Gromyko, the Soviet foreign minister, and warns him that offensive missiles must not be installed on Cuba. Gromyko insists that the USSR is only aiding the 'defensive capabilities' of Cuba. | Kennedy leaves Washington for scheduled campaign speeches in Cleveland and across the West Coast. | Kennedy cancels the remainder of his campaign trip for 'health reasons'. He meets his advisers and orders that a defensive blockade (quarantine) of Cuba should be established immediately to prevent the arrival of Soviet missiles. | General Maxwell Taylor informs Kennedy that a US airstrike could not guarantee to destroy all Soviet missiles in Cuba. |
| **Monday 22 October** | **Tuesday 23 October** | **Wednesday 24 October** | **Thursday 25 October** |
| Kennedy addresses the US on TV. He announces a blockade of Cuba, as offensive missile bases were discovered there. Kennedy also issues a demand for the immediate withdrawal of Soviet missiles. US military forces go to Defence Condition (DEFCON) 3. The US base at Guantanamo Bay (Cuba) is reinforced by marines. | US ships are positioned along the quarantine line (800 miles from Cuba). Khrushchev sends Kennedy a letter, which states that there is a 'serious threat to the peace and security of peoples'. In order to buy time, Kennedy pulls the quarantine line back to 500 miles. | American forces go to DEFCON 2 (one short of war) – the highest ever in US history. Soviet ships sailing with unidentified cargoes to Cuba either slow down or reverse their course. | Kennedy sends Khrushchev a letter blaming the Soviet Union for the crisis. US reconnaissance photographs are shown at the UN General Assembly to prove Soviet military activity in Cuba. |
| **Friday 26 October** | **Saturday 27 October** | | **Sunday 28 October** |
| Kennedy concludes that the quarantine alone will not remove Soviet missiles from Cuba. The CIA reports no halt in the development of missile sites on Cuba. Khrushchev sends another letter to Kennedy proposing to remove the Soviet missiles, if the US lifts the blockade and publicly pledges never to invade Cuba. | Khrushchev proposes trading Soviet missiles on Cuba for US missiles in Turkey. A U-2 spy plane is shot down over Cuba and the pilot is killed. Kennedy is under pressure to take military action. Instead, he responds to Khrushchev's proposal of 26 October by informing the Soviet leader that he will make a statement saying that the US will not invade Cuba if the USSR removes its missiles from Cuba. Kennedy gives a secret assurance to the Soviets that US missiles could soon leave Turkey. | | Khrushchev accepts Kennedy's terms and announces on Radio Moscow that he has agreed to remove the Soviet missiles from Cuba. The crisis is over. |

## The results of the Cuban missile crisis

### The consequences for the leaders

The results of the Cuban missile crisis had different consequences for each of the three leaders – Kennedy, Khrushchev and Castro:

| | |
|---|---|
| **Consequences for Kennedy**<br> | • The crisis gave Kennedy a much-needed foreign policy success, which strengthened his presidency. To avoid humiliating the Soviets, he sensibly ordered 'no boasting, no gloating, not even a claim of victory'.<br><br>• He could claim to have removed the Soviet nuclear threat from the USA's 'backyard' and to have prevented a superpower nuclear exchange.<br><br>• Ten days after the crisis, Kennedy reaped the domestic political rewards at the US Congressional elections when the Democrats won their biggest majority in the Senate for 20 years.<br><br>• Nevertheless, he had pledged not to attempt to remove Castro from Cuba, and so had effectively accepted that, for the foreseeable future, the island would remain under communist control.<br><br>• Kennedy had secretly agreed with the Soviets to remove US missiles from Turkey. This decision, taken without the knowledge of the Turkish government, was not revealed to the American public until 1968. |
| **Consequences for Khrushchev**<br> | • Khrushchev could claim credit for safeguarding Castro's socialist revolution by obtaining the US pledge not to invade Cuba; he called this 'a spectacular success', which had been achieved 'without having to fire a single shot'.<br><br>• He could also argue that Soviet action in Cuba had removed US Jupiter missiles in Turkey (they were quietly removed by the Americans in 1963 on the grounds that they were 'obsolete').<br><br>• Ultimately, Khrushchev had chosen peace over brinkmanship but the Soviet descent (climb downwards) in October 1962 could not be disguised.<br><br>• The Soviet military never forgave Khrushchev. They regarded the Cuban venture as ending in humiliating failure and this was a factor in Khrushchev's removal from office in 1964. |
| **Consequences for Castro**<br> | • Castro was furious with Khrushchev because he had not been consulted by the USSR about the removal of the missiles. He called the Russian leader names and Cuban forces surrounded the Soviet bases for four days.<br><br>• He was also angry because he had expected the Soviets to insist on the removal of the US military base at Guantanamo Bay.<br><br>• Although Castro regarded the October 1962 crisis as a moral defeat for communism, it reinforced his dependence on the USSR, which continued to provide economic aid to Cuba. |

## The easing of tension in 1963

The Cuban missile crisis had brought the superpowers to the brink of direct nuclear confrontation. In the aftermath, both sides recognised that confidence-building measures were needed to reduce Cold War tensions in crisis situations and to limit the likelihood of nuclear war.

Within a year, the USA and the Soviet Union had signed two important initiatives, which would help to achieve this.

### The 'hot-line' agreement, June 1963

The October 1962 crisis had shown the necessity for rapid communication between the superpowers. As a result, it was decided to set up a 'hot-line' telegraph link between the Whitehouse and the Kremlin so that the US and Soviet leaders could contact each other immediately and hold discussions. The aim was to ensure that any superpower misjudgements and misunderstandings could be resolved before a serious crisis situation developed.

President Richard Nixon and the Soviet leader Leonid Brezhnev used the 'hot-line' in 1971 during the India–Pakistan war.

### The Nuclear Test Ban Treaty, August 1963

By October 1958, both superpowers, aware of the positive publicity value, began a voluntary moratorium on nuclear tests, which lasted for almost three years. During this period, a more formal agreement could not be reached because the USSR rejected US demands for rigorous 'on-site' inspections of underground nuclear tests.

In August 1961, the Soviet Union resumed atmospheric tests and the USA followed suit with a new round of underground and atmospheric nuclear detonations. The sobering impact of the Cuban missile crisis led the two superpowers and Britain to sign the Nuclear Test Ban Treaty (1963), which banned them from conducting nuclear tests in the atmosphere, under water or in space. Underground testing was still permitted.

## The beginnings of détente

Chastened by the experience of the Cuban missile crisis, the USA and the USSR made greater efforts to avoid direct confrontation in the future. The superpowers had only just avoided a nuclear war in October 1962, and both sides were keen to establish better relations. This led to a period of US–Soviet détente, which reached a high point in the 1970s.

### Examiners' notes

Here you need to identify the results of the Cuban missile crisis. You should clearly understand the easing of superpower tensions in 1963 – marked by the installation of the 'hotline' and the signing of the Nuclear Test Ban Treaty.

### Essential notes

'Moratorium' means a suspension of an activity.

### Essential notes

'Détente' is a French term that means 'relaxation'. It is frequently used to describe the period of improved East–West relations from 1963 to 1979.

# An unequal friendship: Sino–Soviet relations, 1949–50

## The People's Republic of China, 1949

On October 1 1949, Mao Zedong announced the creation of the People's Republic of China (PRC). The PRC was created following communist success in a bitter civil war. The creation of the PRC altered the balance of power in the Cold War. Officially, Communist Russia was the first state to recognise Mao's communist government, and quickly signed a Treaty of Friendship with China. The US, by contrast, was horrified that communism had triumphed in China. Consequently, US policy in South-East Asia changed dramatically.

## The Treaty of Friendship, Alliance and Mutual Assistance, February 1950

### *Reasons for the treaty*

The PRC was isolated from the West because it was a Communist state. However, there was an obvious ideological affinity between China and Russia. Indeed, Mao described the USSR as 'our best teacher from whom we must learn'. Therefore, in late 1949, Mao travelled to Moscow for face-to-face talks with Stalin, in search of a powerful ally.

Stalin had less to gain from the treaty, but in the aftermath of the Second World War, the Russian economy needed to be rebuilt. Establishing a new trading partner was in the USSR's interest.

### *The terms of the treaty*

Negotiations were slow because China's need for the alliance was greater than Russia's need. Nonetheless, on February 14 1950, the two nations signed the Treaty of Friendship, Alliance and Mutual Assistance.

**Alliance**
The treaty established a military alliance against 'Japanese militarism', by which it meant capitalist nations. It included a guarantee that the USSR would come to China's aid if China was involved in conflicts with any capitalist nation.

**The Treaty of Friendship, Alliance and Mutual Assistance**

**Mutual assistance**
The USSR and China agreed to trade and share knowledge:
• The USSR and China set up a joint stock company to mine in Xinjiang.
• Soviet experts helped to set up and run 141 Chinese business enterprises.
• China recognised the USSR's rights over Outer Mongolia.
• The USSR returned the Manchurian railway to China.

**Friendship**
The USSR granted the following aid to China:
• a loan of $300 million
• equipment for 50 major construction projects.

A summary of the Treaty of Friendship, Alliance and Mutual Assistance

## The significance of the Treaty: The impact on China

The Treaty allowed China to begin economic modernisation:

- There was a six-fold increase in Sino–Soviet trade from 1950–56.

- By 1956, 60 per cent of Chinese trade was conducted with the USSR.

- The USSR educated 9313 Chinese technical experts in top Russian universities.

- Over 38 000 Chinese workers were given vocational training in Siberia.

Through loans, trade and training the treaty laid the foundation for economic development in China.

### *The creation of the China Lobby in the USA*

The proclamation of a communist regime in China sent shockwaves through the USA, leading to a change in US policy. Prior to the establishment of the PRC, the USA had been disengaging from South-East Asia. A government paper published on August 5 1949, stated that the USA had no strategic interest in China. Moreover, as late as January 1950, US Secretary of State, Dean Acheson, announced that the US had no plans to offer military protection from communism to Korea or Taiwan.

However, the Treaty of Friendship led to the emergence of the 'China Lobby'. Republicans and Democrats associated with the China Lobby were obsessed with the question 'Who lost China?' They believed that President Truman had not done enough to ensure the survival of a pro-Western China and that the alliance between China and the USSR gave a new advantage to the Soviet Union in the Cold War. In this way, the Treaty led to renewed interested in China in the USA.

### *The impact on US government policy*

In response to the China Lobby, Truman changed policy, announcing a series of measures designed to stop the spread of communism in South-East Asia. By mid-1950, the US had agreed to the following:

- Military support for Taiwan – the US dispatched its Seventh Fleet to the Taiwan Strait to discourage a Chinese invasion.

- Military aid for the Philippines – in mid-1950, John F. Melby, head of the US Military Aid Mission, agreed support for the Philippine government against communist revolutionaries.

- Military and financial support for the French, who were battling communism in Vietnam.

- Aid and support for South Korea, as North Korea was a communist country and the US government feared that it was planning to invade capitalist South Korea.

- More generally, the 'loss of China' persuaded the US government that they had not done enough to retain the initiative in the Cold War. Consequently, NSC-68 (see page 12) outlined a more active role for the USA in fighting communism in the Cold War

### Essential notes

Following the defeat of Japan at the end of the Second World War, Korea was divided between the communist north and the capitalist south.

### Essential notes

Following the establishment of the PRC, the former government of China retreated to Taiwan, an island off the east coast of China. Mao was determined to invade Taiwan in order to bring the whole of China under communist control.

Map showing Outer Mongolia, Korea and Taiwan

## The consolidation of Sino–Soviet friendship, 1950–4

### The origins of the Korean War

The Korean War was the first test of the new Sino–Soviet alliance. The military campaign against South Korea was agreed between Stalin and North Korea's communist leader Kim Il-Sung. The negotiations were kept secret from Mao.

### *Stalin's aims for war*

Stalin had a series of priorities in the run-up to the Korean War:

> Soviet troops must not meet American troops in battle. If they do, we will risk nuclear attack. China must do most of the fighting.

> We will not give military aid to China. It will be too expensive.

> We do not want to be forced to fight in Korea under the terms of the Treaty of Friendship.

> We must consolidate Communist control of Korea. If we don't, America will take control of North Korea and attack Russia across the Russo-Korean border.

In essence, Stalin wanted to expand communist influence in South-East Asia without involving Russia in a war. Therefore, he needed to force Mao to fight with minimal Russian aid. Stalin achieved this in the following ways:

- He persuaded Kim Il-Sung to attack South Korea, promising Soviet backing.

- Following the entry of UN troops, Mao feared that North Korea would be defeated, leading to a capitalist invasion of China. This forced Mao to enter the war on the side of North Korea. Mao anticipated Soviet help under the terms of the Treaty of Friendship.

- Stalin refused to help, as China was fighting UN forces; the UN was not a capitalist nation, so the terms of the treaty did not apply.

### The Korean War

China's entry into the Korean War was hugely significant. UN troops were held off and, after three years of fighting, hostilities ended with a reassertion of the division of Korea into communist and capitalist nations. This was a partial success for the USSR. The communist regime in North Korea had been consolidated. However, the war had failed to expand communist influence in South-East Asia.

### *The significance of the war for Sino-Soviet relations*

Although Stalin's manipulation forced Mao to enter the Korean War, the conflict consolidated the Sino–Soviet friendship.

The huge cost of the war increased China's dependence on the USSR. The USSR had refused to join the war as China's ally, but had agreed to sell China advanced military hardware. After the war, China turned to the USSR for aid, to help to rebuild their war-shattered economy.

For Russia, the war had proved China's worth as an ally. Stalin acknowledged that China played a crucial role in acting as a buffer between UN troops and the Soviet border.

Following the Korean War, there were two further Sino–Soviet agreements, in the 1953 and 1954 deals. The USSR agreed to:

- a significant package of aid for China's first Five-Year Plan, including a bigger loan than had been agreed in 1950
- help China build power plants
- hand over the Lushan naval base to China, located on the border between the two countries
- increase trade with China.

### The significance of the war for the USA

The USA was concerned by the Korean War. It demonstrated the potential power of an alliance between the USSR and China. China's willingness to fight alongside other communist nations also made any kind of alliance with the USA impossible.

### Confrontation over Taiwan

After the communist victory in the Chinese Civil War, nationalist forces set up their own government in Taiwan, which was extremely important to Mao for two reasons:

- He was concerned that Taiwan could be used as a US base in a future war between China and the US.
- Mao wanted to unite China under communist leadership.

As a result, Mao launched two unsuccessful attempts to take Taiwan by force. The first, which was from 1954–5 was significant because of the response of the superpowers:

- In the USA, Congress moved quickly to defend Taiwan. In September, US military leaders advised Eisenhower to use nuclear weapons to defend Taiwan. Eisenhower refused, but in December 1954 the US and Taiwan signed a Mutual Defence Treaty, guaranteeing Taiwan's independence. The US response demonstrated ongoing hostility between the USA and China.

- In the USSR, Khrushchev publically agreed to retaliate against the US if China was invaded or bombed by US forces. In private he made it clear that he did not want to be involved. The Soviet response was significant because it showed that the USSR was unwilling to help China to achieve its military goals. It also indicated that Khrushchev was worried that Mao's ill-judged foreign policy would lead to nuclear war.

### Essential notes

Following Stalin's rise to power, Russia's economy had been organised through a series of Five-Year Plans. This became the model for other communist countries, and in 1953, Mao launched his First Five-Year Plan.

### Essential notes

The Chinese Civil War was fought between the nationalist forces of the Guomindang and the Communist Party.

### Essential notes

Following Stalin's death in 1953, there was a brief power struggle, which resulted in Khrushchev assuming leadership of the USSR (see pages 30–3).

## Deterioration of Sino–Soviet relations, 1954–8

Following Stalin's death, the Sino–Soviet relationship enjoyed a brief 'honeymoon period'. Khrushchev, as the new Soviet premier, agreed to more economic aid. He also agreed, personally, to visit China. Still, tensions between the two powers began to emerge.

The period 1954–7 was significant because of the growing erosion of trust between the USSR and China. During this period, China began to emerge as an ideological rival to the USSR: it was no longer clear that the USSR alone led the communist world. Equally, Mao was less inclined to follow Khrushchev because of his reluctance to back China's strategic aims in Taiwan and his reluctance to stand up to the USA in the Cold War.

The personal relationship between Mao and Khrushchev also suffered because of Mao's willingness to snub Khrushchev and disagree with him publically. However, China was still dependent on Soviet aid, and the global authority of the USSR was strengthened by the Sino–Soviet alliance. Therefore, the two remained allies.

### Deterioration during 1958

In 1958, Mao launched a new policy which was a clear rejection of the USSR's model of economic development. Indeed, he claimed that the 'Great Leap Forward' was superior to the USSR's Five-Year Plans. The Great Leap Forward was a turning point in China's relationship with the USSR because it demonstrated to the world that Mao was willing to forge his own path, increasingly independent of the USSR.

### *The Great Leap Forward*

The Great Leap Forward was a rejection of the Soviet model of economic development. Whereas the USSR stressed the role of expertise and the working class in developing the economy, the Great Leap Forward was based on the enthusiasm of the peasants.

Mao was increasingly convinced that Khrushchev was not a real revolutionary. Instead, he believed that Khrushchev was an administrator concerned with organisation and not with change. By initiating the Great Leap Forward, Mao was consciously distancing himself from the USSR and undermining Khrushchev's leadership of the communist world.

### *Further deterioration during 1958*

The Great Leap Forward was a signal of Mao's self-confidence and his willingness to act independently of the USSR. Differences over Taiwan further convinced Mao that Khrushchev lacked revolutionary spirit and led to Mao's deliberate humiliation of Khrushchev during his second visit to China.

### Essential notes

Khrushchev's 'Secret Speech' of April 1956 (see page 30) was given to the Communist Party Congress. In this speech, Khrushchev criticised Stalin's style of government.

### Essential notes

Mao's Great Leap Forward (1958–62) was an attempt to catch up with Western economies in terms of the production of raw materials such as steel. In practice, Mao encouraged every household to make steel in their own furnaces. This resulted in a large amount of steel being produced, but it was of very low quality.

### *China's national and military interests*

During 1958, differences emerged between the USSR and China over nuclear arms and the position of Taiwan.

In July 1958, Khrushchev proposed joint Russian–Chinese control over China's nuclear programme. In practice, this would mean that China's nuclear weapons could only be used with Soviet authorisation. Mao believed that this was patronising. He also felt that the USSR was being slow to share its own nuclear secrets.

In September, China began a second bombardment of Taiwan. Khrushchev refused to support this as he feared that confrontation between China and Taiwan could drag their allies, the USSR and the USA, into a nuclear war.

Initially, Khrushchev attempted to persuade Mao to end the attack on Taiwan by agreeing to share Russia's nuclear secrets with China. He even offered to send China a sample bomb. However, in January 1959, Khrushchev changed his mind, proposing a Pacific 'atom-free zone', which would mean China abandoning its nuclear programme.

The Second Taiwan Crisis convinced Mao that Khrushchev could not be relied on to advance China's strategic interests. Furthermore, the crisis confirmed Mao's belief that Khrushchev was in favour of compromise with capitalism rather than revolution. Khrushchev, on the other hand, believed that Mao acted rashly, risking nuclear war in his desire to conquer Taiwan.

### *Personalities*

In August 1958, the personal relationship between Mao and Khrushchev was further strained. During Khrushchev's first visit to China, Mao set out to deliberately humiliate the Soviet leader. He organised a photo-opportunity at his personal swimming pool knowing that Khrushchev could not swim. Mao swum confidently before the cameras while Khrushchev floundered in a rubber ring. For Khrushchev, this publicity stunt demonstrated Mao's capricious (unpredictable) nature.

### Sino–Soviet relations in 1958

By the end of 1958, Russia and China remained allies. China had no other major allies and therefore depended on the USSR for aid. Equally, Russia still hoped that its alliance with China would give it the upper hand against the US in the Cold War as it united two extremely powerful armies.

Nonetheless, 1958 was a turning point in Sino–Soviet relations. Mao's actions signalled his desire to contest Khrushchev's leadership of the communist world. Equally, the relationship between the two leaders became increasingly strained.

The USA was largely ignorant of the tensions in the relationship between the two communist powers. Therefore, it did little to capitalise on these growing tensions.

**Examiners' notes**

The quality of your written communication can affect your mark. Poor grammar and spelling can move your mark from the top to the bottom of a level. For this reason, it is worth taking time to learn how to spell names such as Khrushchev and even Mao (a surprising number of students misspell his name 'Moa').

**Essential notes**

Mao was highly critical of bureaucracy. He compared revolutionaries, who were idealists and people of action, with bureaucrats, who he believed put administration before ideology. Bureaucrats were therefore more likely to compromise with capitalism.

## Sino–Soviet confrontation, 1959–69

### Reasons for further deterioration in the Sino–Soviet relationship

Further deterioration of the Sino–Soviet relationship resulted from personal differences, ideological division and strategic issues.

### *Personal differences and political rivalries*

Khrushchev's second visit to China occurred in 1959, and was intended to celebrate the 10th anniversary of the Chinese Revolution. Mao used this opportunity to snub the Russian leader in public. On Khrushchev's arrival, no guard of honour met him, and no microphone was provided. At their meeting, Khrushchev and Mao openly insulted each other. In private, Khrushchev made fun of the Chinese, rhyming Chinese names with Russian obscenities. Mao was outraged.

In May 1960, Mao took special pleasure in beating the Russians to the top of Mount Everest. The Russians may have been the first to launch a satellite into space, but Chinese propaganda made a big thing of the fact that Chinese mountaineers had reached the summit of Everest ahead of the Russians.

In July 1960, Khrushchev responded to the continuing difficulties in the relationship with China by withdrawing the Russian experts who were helping with the Great Leap Forward.

In 1963, Mao took his revenge by publicising Khrushchev's backdown over the Cuban Missile Crisis. This was humiliating for Khrushchev, as it demonstrated his lack of resolve when dealing with the US.

### *Ideological division*

During the late 1950s, ideological division between the two communist powers became increasingly evident. In 1959, Khrushchev publically criticised Mao's Great Leap Forward. In 1960, Mao responded by calling Khrushchev a 'revisionist', and no longer on the true path of communism.

In 1961, Khrushchev announced an important new doctrine. He maintained that class struggle was over in Russia; therefore the USSR represented all of the people of Russia, not just the working class. Mao argued that this was a betrayal of communism, an ideology that focused on the interests of the working class.

The ideological rift deepened in 1964, when Mao described Khrushchev's communism as 'phoney'. He said that the USSR, under Khrushchev, had become a bureaucratic and consumerist regime that was prepared to compromise with the West.

### *Strategic and military issues*

The Sino–Indian Border Conflict of 1962 exposed important divisions between the USSR and China. Rather than back his communist ally, Khrushchev publically criticised China's war involvement, claiming that the dispute should have been settled peacefully. He signalled support for India by sending aid worth $800 million. Mao was enraged. Similarly, Khrushchev backed Indonesia during the Sino–Indonesian disputes of 1959–62 by sending massive Soviet military aid to China's enemy.

### Essential notes

Khrushchev criticised Mao's Great Leap Forward by pointing out that the policy had been wasteful and had led to famine.

### Essential notes

The Sino–Indian Border Conflict emerged from disputes between China and India over their border in the Himalayas. The Sino–Indonesian disputes stemmed from Indonesia's attempt to deny civil rights to the Chinese population in Indonesia.

In 1964, Khrushchev was dismayed at China's first successful nuclear weapons test. It was rumoured that Khrushchev even initiated a plot to overthrow Mao in the wake of the weapons test.

### Sino–Soviet relations after Khrushchev

In 1964, Khrushchev was removed from power in the USSR. The new Soviet leader, Leonid Brezhnev, attempted to establish a working relationship with Mao. However, in 1965 Mao launched a new ideological campaign: the Cultural Revolution.

During the Cultural Revolution, Mao outlined a new ideological insight. He argued that the USA and the USSR were 'the global cities', and China and the Third World were 'the global countryside'. This was significant because Mao argued that the workers in the 'countryside' were the true revolutionaries, whereas 'city' people were decadent bureaucrats.

In March 1966, the USSR and China finally ended diplomatic and trading relations. By the summer of 1966, there was minimal contact between the two governments, who were only prepared to collaborate in order to get arms from the Soviet Union to Vietnam, via China.

### Full-scale confrontation, 1968–9

The Cultural Revolution relied on a new breed of soldier known as the Red Guards. The Red Guards intensified the problems between China and Russia, signalling their contempt for Russia by crossing the Sino–Soviet border into Soviet territory in 1968. Brezhnev was unsure about the significance of these invasions, but responded with force. By 1968, 15 divisions of the Russian army were stationed on the Sino–Soviet border.

On 2 March 1969, the Red Guards occupied the island of Zhen Bao, known to the Russians as Damanskii. The island's status was disputed, with both sides claiming it as part of their territory. Small-scale fighting broke out immediately, with a massive Soviet counter-attack on March 15.

The fighting was short-lived, but the Chinese government was horrified to hear that Russian diplomats were informally talking to the USA about a series of nuclear strikes against China. Mao took this very seriously and began moving key personnel into nuclear bunkers.

On September 18, crisis was averted, as senior ministers from both sides agreed to respect each other's borders.

### Significance of the Sino–Soviet split for superpower relations

The Sino–Soviet split weakened the Soviet Union, thus providing an opportunity for the USA.

The split between the two communist powers indicated that there were different interpretations of applying communism. Communist countries around the world could choose to follow China rather than the USSR, so the USSR lost ideological and moral authority in the communist world.

The public dispute between China and the USSR alerted the US government to divisions in the communist world. As a result, US President Nixon began to consider developing a Sino–US relationship to exploit difficulties between China and the USSR.

### Essential notes

After the failure of the Great Leap Forward, Mao had been partially sidelined by other senior figures. The Cultural Revolution was a period of turmoil, initiated by Mao in an attempt to reassert his dominance over China. For example, Mao appealed directly to China's youth, encouraging them to form militia units known as the Red Guard. These units were at the forefront of the Cultural Revolution.

### Examiners' notes

If you are faced with the question 'Why was there a breakdown in Sino–Soviet relations in the years 1954–69?' it is worth considering the question thematically. For example, you could distinguish between personal, ideological and strategic causes of the deterioration. Be sure to draw conclusions about which factor was most significant in the breakdown of relations. Consider that strategic and military issues remained a continual problem, whereas personal differences were less significant after Khrushchev's fall in 1964.

## Launching 'ping-pong' diplomacy

Between 1949 and the late 1960s, the USA was China's 'Number One Enemy'. However, secret negotiations, and later, public meetings developed a working relationship between the two powers, which altered the balance of the Cold War.

### The USA and China, 1949–69

The USA had backed the Guomindang (Mao's nationalist enemy) in the 1930s. In 1949, the USA was on the verge of a 'Red Scare' and was horrified by the creation of a new communist power. In fact, for many years, the USA refused to recognise the People's Republic of China, and US Presidents refused to call China by its proper name, preferring to call the communist regime 'Red China'. The relationship worsened during the Korean War as US and Chinese troops fought each other. During the 1950s and 1960s, there was no trade, no diplomatic links, and no sporting competition between the two nations.

During the early 1960s, President Kennedy discussed exploiting the Sino–Soviet split. However, this was ruled out by US involvement in Vietnam. The first real moves towards establishing a relationship between the two countries took place in 1969.

### Motives for Sino–US rapprochement

Chinese motives:

- Mao was worried about reports of a pre-emptive Soviet nuclear strike.

- In 1969, China had very few allies as, during the Cultural Revolution, China withdrew its ambassadors from most countries. By 1969, China only had three real allies: France, Pakistan and Albania.

- Mao hoped that an alliance with the USA could be used to confront the USSR, thus forcing it to accept an expansion of China's borders.

US motives:

- President Nixon hoped that he could persuade China to put pressure on the Vietcong to negotiate a peaceful settlement in Vietnam.

- Nixon wanted to exploit the Sino–Soviet split by using a relationship with China to put pressure on the USSR to compromise with the West.

- The Vietnam War had demonstrated that US military power was not as effective as had been hoped. Nixon wanted to make up for US military failures through new strategic alliances.

- Nixon wanted to stop a Soviet invasion of China because he did not want China to become a Russian satellite.

- Nixon hoped that friendship with China would allow the USA to focus its entire nuclear arsenal on the USSR.

### Essential notes

The 'Red Scare' refers to two periods in US history during which elements within the government stoked public fears about the threat of communism. The Second Red Scare was, in part, brought about by the emergence of a communist government in China.

### Essential notes

Richard Nixon took office as President in 1969 and served until 1974. Henry Kissinger served as Nixon's National Security Advisor, and then as his Secretary of State.

## Key events in Sino–US 'ping-pong' diplomacy

Negotiations between the USA and China were known as 'ping-pong' diplomacy. This is because one of the first signs of friendship between the nations was a ping-pong match played by the US and Chinese national ping-pong teams. For Mao, ping-pong was hugely significant. In fact, during the Cultural Revolution, he encouraged Red Guards to sing 'The Ping-Pong Song', which likened table tennis to guerrilla warfare.

Key events in Sino–US 'ping-pong' diplomacy were as follows:

| Year | Month | Event |
|------|-------|-------|
| 1969 | July | Nixon relaxes trade and travel restrictions to China. |
| | | The USA recognises the People's Republic of China. |
| | | Nixon initiates a secret dialogue with Mao through Pakistan. |
| 1971 | April | Mao invites the US ping-pong team to play an international match in China. |
| | July | Nixon's National Security Advisor, Henry Kissinger, visits China secretly to arrange a presidential visit for the subsequent year. |
| | October | The USA backs the PRC's entry into the UN. |

## Problems with 'ping-pong' diplomacy

Until mid-1971, negotiations between the USA and China were kept secret. Both sides had good reasons for secrecy.

### National pride

There were no guarantees that negotiations would be fruitful. A public snub from one leader to the other could irreparably damage negotiations. In 1954, Dulles, US Secretary of State, had publically refused to shake hands with the Chinese Prime Minister, Zhou Enlai, causing great embarrassment. As a result, Kissinger had to assure the Chinese government that Nixon would shake hands with their senior members.

### Domestic opinion

China and the USA used propaganda against each other extensively between 1949 and 1969. For example, in China, US citizens were routinely represented as vampires; in the USA, China was known as the 'Yellow Peril'. Both sides had to be careful how negotiations were presented to the public.

### Taiwan

The USA had a long-standing commitment to defend the rights of Taiwan against the PRC. Mao's central foreign policy aim was to avoid the renewed domination of China by foreign powers, which Russia might have liked. This basic disagreement posed significant problems for a Sino–US agreement.

In spite of these difficulties, Kissinger and Zhou Enlai agreed on a presidential visit during February 1972.

### Examiners' notes

Section A questions require focused analysis for marks in the top levels. For this reason, it is important that your answer is relevant to the question rather than extensive in coverage. When answering a question on 'ping-pong' diplomacy it may not be necessary to discuss all of the events on the timeline. Think carefully about the question you are tackling and select only examples that will help to further your argument.

## Sino–US relations, 1972–6

Nixon's visit to China in 1972 began a new era of Sino–US relations. It was a bold move designed by Nixon to change the dynamics of the Cold War. Nixon and Kissinger wanted to move away from a bipolar world of superpower confrontation to a multipolar world in which different powers dealt with each other by negotiation. This policy was known as triangular diplomacy. In practice, Nixon attempted to foster friendly relations with the USSR and China, and in so doing played the two powers off each other.

Following Nixon's resignation, President Ford continued Nixon's policy of triangular diplomacy, as shown in the diagram.

Nixon's aim was to make the Cold War relations more stable by creating a three-way relationship between the USA, the USSR and China, rather than having a two-way confrontation.

Nixon anticipated that the USSR would be worried by a potential Sino–US alliance and that in response the USSR would maintain friendly relations with the US.

Nixon offered Mao support in China's battle to stay independent of the USSR. Nixon reasoned that an independent China was better for the USA than a China that was a mere Soviet satellite.

The USA

The USSR          China

The USA, the USSR and China – a three-way relationship

### Nixon's trip to China, 1972

In February 1972, Nixon flew to China. The trip was a risk because there was no guarantee that Mao would agree to see the US President. However, Mao was genuinely excited about meeting a world leader and the two men met and established a good working relationship.

As a result of the meeting, the two leaders published the Shanghai Communiqué of 28 February 1972. The Communiqué:

- acknowledged substantial disagreements over Korea, Vietnam and Taiwan

- committed the USA and China to a relationship of peaceful co-existence based on mutual respect

- stated that the USA and China would seek to normalise the relationship by 1976, meaning that they would establish formal diplomatic links

- pledged that the two powers would work together to resist any country that sought to dominate South-East Asia – this part of the Communiqué was an implicit reference to the USSR

- committed the USA and China to increase co-operation and trade.

Nixon's trip did not fully normalise the relationship between the USA and China. It was, however, a highly significant event that shocked the US public and the leaders of the USSR, changing the dynamics of the Cold War relationship.

## The impact on the USSR

Nixon's visit to China caused great anxiety at the top of the Soviet government. Moreover, it forced the Soviet government to maintain friendly and co-operative relations with the USA, as they feared the emergence of an anti-Soviet Sino–US alliance:

- As early as 1969, the USSR had been monitoring US interest in China, fearful of a Sino–US alliance.

- As a result, the USSR had to divide its military resources and plan for 'a war on two fronts' – a war in Europe with NATO forces and a war in the East with China.

- At the same time, Soviet leaders were aware that the USA's new friendship with China meant that the USA could now focus its defensive strategy on the USSR.

- Soviet leaders were concerned that China might persuade the USA to abandon détente.

Nixon's triangular diplomacy bore fruit immediately. Three months after his visit to China, Nixon attended the Moscow summit of May 1972. This was the most successful summit of the Cold War to date. The USSR agreed to sign the SALT I treaties and the Basic Principles Agreement, which effectively normalised the relationship between the two superpowers. Though the Soviet leaders never acknowledged that Nixon's visit to China was behind their willingness to negotiate, senior officials in Nixon's administration certainly believed that triangular diplomacy had played a role in the success of the summit.

## Sino–US relations after Nixon

After Nixon's resignation in 1974, President Ford tried to follow Nixon's approach to China, aiming for normalisation by 1976. Kissinger made a trip to China in 1975, with the aim of reaching agreement over Taiwan and offering co-operation on military and intelligence matters. However, Kissinger failed to reach agreement on any of these issues.

Ford visited China in December 1975. His position was much weaker than Nixon's had been, as he was unpopular with the US public and did not enjoy the support of Congress. As a result, he was not in a position to compromise on any of the sensitive issues. The visit did little to hasten normalisation, but it did consolidate the working relationship between the two governments, which had been initiated by Nixon's visit to China in 1972.

### Examiners' notes

'Ping-pong' diplomacy was related to a bigger foreign policy initiative known as 'détente' (see page 51). Although this book treats 'ping-pong' diplomacy and 'détente' separately, you should be aware of the links between the different aspects of the course. In fact, US–Chinese relations have a bearing on nuclear rivalry as well as détente.

## The origins of détente, 1969–72

### The nature of détente

The exact definition of détente is disputed. Broadly, it refers to a period in which the USA and USSR attempted to reach general agreement on arms reduction and trade relations. Détente was also characterised by summit meetings between senior figures and a reduction in hostile propaganda. However, détente did not include any attempt to resolve the ideological differences between the two superpowers.

### Nixon and détente

Nixon became the US President in 1969. Détente was one of his key policy objectives and is therefore dated to the beginning of his presidency.

### The superpowers and détente

The superpowers were united in pursuing détente in order to avoid a nuclear war. Between 1963 and 1969, the USSR began to close the 'missile gap' with the United States. By 1969, the arms race had created a situation in which a full-scale nuclear war would lead to 'mutually assured destruction' (MAD). Both sides recognised that it was vital to avoid nuclear war. In addition, the two superpowers each had independent reasons for seeking an accommodation in the early 1970s.

### Reasons for the USA to pursue détente

### Vietnam

The Nixon government's primary objective was the withdrawal of US troops from Vietnam. The Vietnam War had weakened the moral authority of the United States as leader of the free world, and was also extremely expensive. In 1969 alone, the war cost the US government $30 billion. Nixon hoped that withdrawal could be achieved, in part, by improving relations with the USSR, who had supported the Vietcong since Brezhnev came to power in late 1964.

### Economics

By 1970, the 'long post-war boom' was coming to an end:

- Inflation reached 6% in 1970.

- Unemployment rose to more than 5% in the early 1970s.

- The early 1970s witnessed the end of the Bretton Woods currency system – a system that had fixed international exchange rates. The collapse of Bretton Woods and the introduction of free-floating currencies (currencies without fixed relative values), made international trade less stable, leading to economic difficulties throughout the West.

Détente offered a partial solution to the USA's economic concerns, as it had the potential to create a reduction in defence spending and greater trade with the USSR.

### Essential notes

Leonid Brezhnev became Secretary-General of the Russian Communist Party in 1964 and held this position until his death in 1982.

### Examiners' notes

Examiners are looking for a comprehensive understanding of the topic. For example, they will be impressed if you can apply technical economic terms such as 'inflation', accurately.

### Kissinger's realpolitik

The Nixon government, particularly Henry Kissinger, was committed to 'realpolitik'. Détente was an expression of realpolitik, and focused on practical issues such as arms reduction, rather than resolving ideological differences.

### Normalisation

Kissinger believed that the process of negotiation could 'normalise' the relationship between the USA and the USSR. Essentially, Kissinger believed that détente could create a framework in which the two superpowers could work, preventing erratic behaviour on the part of the USSR.

### Reasons for the USSR to pursue détente

### Economics

The economy of the USSR was roughly a sixth the size of that of the USA. There were increasing demands for consumer goods from the Russian population, which their economy could not fulfil. Détente allowed Russian leaders to ease their economic problems by reducing defence spending and encouraging loans and trade from the West.

### Nuclear parity

The economy of the USSR could not produce nuclear weapons as effectively as that of the USA. By the end of 1969, the USA's nuclear arsenal consisted of 28 200 warheads, whereas the USSR held only 11 000. Détente offered the USSR the possibility of achieving nuclear parity (a roughly equal balance between the nuclear arsenals of the East and the West) through treaties that limited the nuclear stockpiles of both countries.

### China

The deterioration of Sino–Soviet relations, and the USA's increasing willingness to negotiate with China, caused the *Politburo* to fear an anti-Soviet alliance between the USA and China. Détente was an attempt to diffuse this by establishing a working relationship with the USA.

### The Third World

Brezhnev was committed to extending Soviet influence in the Third World. This risked destabilising the relationship between the USA and the USSR. Détente was an attempt to placate the USA and therefore extend influence in the Third World without risking further conflict.

**Essential notes**

Realpolitik meant the USA maintaining realistic goals in their dealings with the USSR and China, rather than pursuing an ideological struggle between capitalism and communism.

**Examiners' notes**

Analysis is important to exam success. Categorisation is one aspect of analysis. Here, the USSR's reasons for pursuing détente have been broken down into four categories. In order to access the higher levels of the mark scheme, you should approach essay writing in the same way, with an organised structure and detailed development of each of your categories. You should then weigh up the relative importance of each category and reach a substantiated conclusion.

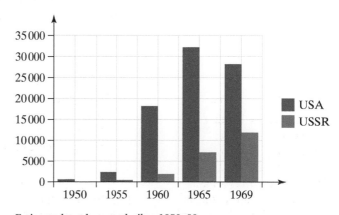

Estimated nuclear stockpiles, 1950–69

|  | USSR | USA |
|---|---|---|
| Missile launchers | 1618 | 1054 |
| Submarine-based launchers | 740 | 656 |

**Essential notes**

An anti-ballistic missile shield is a collection of missiles which are designed to intercept and destroy incoming missiles before they reach their target. The USA had effective anti-ballistic missile technology, whereas the USSR were struggling. Consequently, the Anti-Ballistic Missile Treaty worked in the USSR's favour because it stopped an anti-ballistic missile arms race that they could not win.

# The key features of détente, 1970–75

## The Moscow Summit, 1972

At the Moscow Summit of May 1972, Nixon and Brezhnev set out the basis of the new relationship between their countries. SALT I, the culmination of the Strategic Arms Limitations Talks, was at the heart of the meeting.

## SALT I, 1972

Negotiations between the USA and the USSR on the topic of arms limitation started in November 1969. Talks were held in private, to allow both superpowers to share sensitive information. In May 1972, Nixon and Brezhnev signed two agreements collectively known as SALT I. This agreement contained two main elements, as follows.

### The Anti-Ballistic Missile Treaty

- This restricted the USA and USSR to two anti-ballistic missile shields each.

- Each anti-ballistic missile shield was restricted to 100 missiles.

- The further development of anti-ballistic missile technology was restricted. An Oversight Commission was established to enforce this aspect of the treaty.

### The Interim Agreement on Offensive Missiles

The Interim Agreement limited the number of missile launchers as follows: The Interim Agreement was due to last for five years in anticipation of a full agreement to be drawn up by 1977.

SALT I was significant because it changed the relationship between the superpowers. The treaty signalled that they were willing to work together to limit the production and stockpiling of nuclear weapons, rather than engage in an arms race.

## The Basic Principles Agreement

The Moscow Summit also agreed on the Basic Principles Agreement, which was made up of 12 fundamental principles, designed to underpin superpower relations. These included an acceptance that the superpowers would co-exist peacefully, recognise each other as equals, exercise restraint at times of crisis, and avoid confrontation.

The meeting also agreed on a Joint Commercial Commission, which negotiated trade deals between the two superpowers.

The Basic Principles Agreement was significant because, for the first time, it introduced a series of rules governing most aspects of the relationship between the two superpowers. In this sense, it made the relationship more stable.

## European Ostpolitik

European nations on both sides of the Iron Curtain were involved in their own form of détente. This was known as Ostpolitik. In practice, it involved European governments working together to address the problems created by a divided Europe. West Germany was particularly committed to Ostpolitik.

During 1970 and 1971, the East and West German governments negotiated the Berlin Agreement, which guaranteed the borders of West Germany. This was significant because, prior to the agreement, the Eastern Bloc had refused to, formally, recognise the existence of West Germany. Ostpolitik was important for détente, as it further stabilised superpower relations.

## The Helsinki Accords, 1975

The Helsinki Accords of 1975 set out a comprehensive framework governing relations between Eastern and Western Europe. The agreement tackled three aspects of European politics, which became known as 'baskets'. The Helsinki Accords were significant because they established a framework for managing a divided Europe.

| | |
|---|---|
| **Basket 1: Security issues** | European states pledged to respect one another's sovereignty. In practice, this meant that European states would not interfere in one another's internal affairs. European states promised to respect one another's borders, and they accepted the possibility that borders might change through peaceful negotiation. |
| **Basket 2: Economic, cultural, scientific, and environmental Issues** | European states pledged to co-operate on matters of mutual interest and to foster good trading relations across Europe. To this end, they agreed to share Western technology with the East. |
| **Basket 3: Human rights** | European states pledged to respect the human rights of their citizens. They also pledged to relax travel restrictions across Europe. |

## The unlooked-for significance of the Helsinki Accords

The Helsinki Accords led to unforeseen problems for Eastern Europe and the USSR. The economic co-operation agreed to in Basket 2 highlighted the inferiority of communist economies. Goods produced by the economies of Western Europe were more sophisticated and of a higher quality. In this sense, the baskets led to 'ideological subversion'. That is to say, they led citizens in the Eastern Bloc and the USSR to question the efficiency of the communist economy, undermining the legitimacy of communist rule.

Basket 3 also led to unforeseen problems. Travel restrictions from West to East were relaxed. This led to the establishment of business relationships and friendships that crossed the Iron Curtain. Through these contacts, citizens of the Eastern Bloc and the USSR learned about the culture of Western Europe. Specifically, they learnt about a system in which there was considerable freedom of the press, freedom of speech and religion, and political democracy. In this way, citizens of Eastern Europe discovered a more attractive alternative to communist rule.

The Helsinki Accords, and the trade and travel that were initiated, clearly played a significant role in undermining the legitimacy of the Communist regimes in Eastern Europe and the USSR.

**Essential notes**

The Berlin Agreement, 'guaranteed the borders of West Germany' – that is to say powers in the Eastern bloc agreed not to invade West German territory.

**Essential notes**

The three baskets of the Helsinki Accords were pledges only and could not be legally enforced. This is one reason why they were termed 'baskets' rather than laws.

**Examiners' notes**

The Helsinki Accords had a series of unintended consequences. Do not confuse the consequences of an act or policy with the intentions that led to it. Events often have unexpected consequences.

## The reality and success of détente, 1973–6

Between 1973 and 1976, changes in the international economy had a profound effect on détente. The difference in economic performance between the two superpowers led to a change in the dynamics of détente, with criticism of the policy emerging on both sides.

### The oil price shock

In 1973, the OPEC Crisis destabilised the international economy. In October 1973, in response to the Yom Kippur War, OPEC launched a complete oil embargo against Israel's allies, including the USA. The crisis led to a four-fold increase in the price of oil within a year.

### The economic realities of détente in the West

Following the OPEC Crisis, Western economies rebounded quickly. In the West, countries responded to the oil crisis with innovation and reform:

- They created more efficient engines and tapped new sources of fuel.

- France spearheaded the creation of the G7 group, comprising finance ministers from the USA, Britain, Japan, West Germany, Italy, Canada and France. Negotiations between the members of the G7 brought about renewed economic stability at an international level, therefore compensating for the failure of Bretton Woods.

- Between 1974 and 1978, there was a return to oil price stability. This formed a foundation for further economic growth.

The renewed economic strength of the West, cut the need for détente in the eyes of the US government.

### The economic realities of détente in the East

From 1945 to 1970, the Soviet economy had performed relatively well, reducing the wealth gap between themselves and the USA. However, from 1970, the economy of the USSR began a marked decline.

By 1980, the Gross Domestic Product (GDP) of the USSR was only 37% of the GDP of the USA. There were three main causes of this decline.

- Brezhnev ordered the end of economic liberalisation in the Soviet Union, and a return to central planning. These traditional methods were inefficient and failed to promote or sustain economic growth.

- The USSR had borrowed money from the West in the early 1970s. A rise in interest rates in the later 1970s hit the USSR hard.

- Critics of détente in the United States tried to limit the trade agreements between America and the USSR. Congress introduced the Jackson–Vanik amendment in 1974, making trade between the two superpowers conditional on the protection of human rights in the USSR. In response, the USSR pulled out of the trade deal. This denied the USSR access to US technology.

| Year | Industrial growth in the USSR |
|------|-------------------------------|
| 1964 | 8.2% |
| 1973 | 5.7% |
| 1979 | 1.0% |

## The significance of the economic imbalance

Economic decline in the East made détente more desirable for Soviet leaders for two reasons:

- Détente slowed the arms race, which the struggling Soviet economy could no longer afford.

- Détente facilitated trade with the West, which allowed the USSR access to cheap Western goods.

At the same time as the USSR's economy was in decline, the growing strength of the US economy led to an imbalance of power between East and West. It was no accident that the USA became less committed to détente as the economic imbalance moved in favour of the USA.

## How successful was détente to 1976?

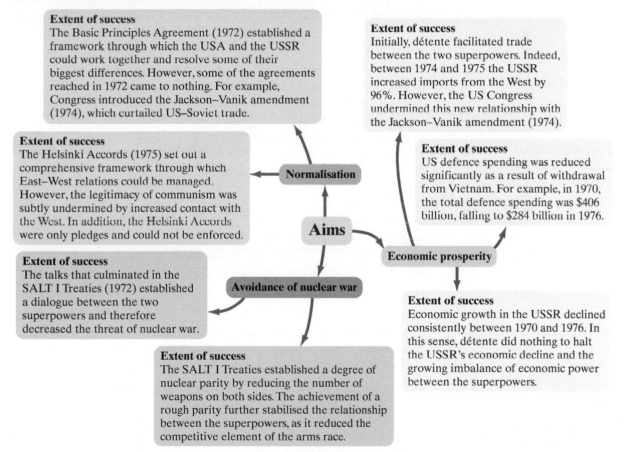

**Extent of success**
The Basic Principles Agreement (1972) established a framework through which the USA and the USSR could work together and resolve some of their biggest differences. However, some of the agreements reached in 1972 came to nothing. For example, Congress introduced the Jackson–Vanik amendment (1974), which curtailed US–Soviet trade.

**Extent of success**
Initially, détente facilitated trade between the two superpowers. Indeed, between 1974 and 1975 the USSR increased imports from the West by 96%. However, the US Congress undermined this new relationship with the Jackson–Vanik amendment (1974).

**Extent of success**
The Helsinki Accords (1975) set out a comprehensive framework through which East–West relations could be managed. However, the legitimacy of communism was subtly undermined by increased contact with the West. In addition, the Helsinki Accords were only pledges and could not be enforced.

**Extent of success**
US defence spending was reduced significantly as a result of withdrawal from Vietnam. For example, in 1970, the total defence spending was $406 billion, falling to $284 billion in 1976.

**Normalisation**

**Aims**

**Economic prosperity**

**Extent of success**
The talks that culminated in the SALT I Treaties (1972) established a dialogue between the two superpowers and therefore decreased the threat of nuclear war.

**Avoidance of nuclear war**

**Extent of success**
Economic growth in the USSR declined consistently between 1970 and 1976. In this sense, détente did nothing to halt the USSR's economic decline and the growing imbalance of economic power between the superpowers.

**Extent of success**
The SALT I Treaties established a degree of nuclear parity by reducing the number of weapons on both sides. The achievement of a rough parity further stabilised the relationship between the superpowers, as it reduced the competitive element of the arms race.

Détente until 1976

Overall, détente was successful in stabilising superpower relations. However, the American people remained suspicious of co-operation with the USSR. The economic consequences of détente were much more favourable for the USA than for the USSR, leading to a growing imbalance of power between the superpowers. In this sense, the successes of détente were partially responsible for its failure.

## Critics of détente

### Critics of détente in the USA, 1970–75

Détente faced harsh criticism from within the USA. Some argued that détente was essentially an amoral policy, which ignored the USSR's violations of human rights. Criticisms began in 1970 following the intervention of the Moscow Human Rights Committee, headed by Andrei Sakharov. The committee established contact with Amnesty International in order to monitor human rights abuses in the USSR. This caused the US government much embarrassment because it highlighted continuing human rights violations on the part of the USSR at a time when the USA was seeking to improve relations.

Similarly, Russian novelist Aleksandr Solzhenitsyn – based in the USA after his exile from the USSR in 1974 – criticised détente, arguing that the policy should not continue while there was still political repression on the part of the USSR. Solzhenitsyn's criticism was taken up by 24 Senators from both political parties.

George Meany, a union leader, argued that détente was the new appeasement. He argued that détente allowed the USSR to grow in strength, unchallenged by the USA. As a result, his union refused to load grain onto ships bound for the USSR.

Theodore Draper, a US historian, also likened détente to appeasement. He went further, arguing that trade with the USA allowed the USSR to grow stronger through cheap imports of grain and US technology. Moreover, he claimed that America got practically nothing from the deal except 'a smile from Brezhnev'.

The SALT I Agreements also provoked fierce criticism. Prior to SALT I, some critics argued, the US had been winning the Cold War. SALT I, they argued, swapped US pre-eminence for parity between the superpowers. Some went further, arguing that détente was handing victory in the Cold War to the USSR.

### The 1976 presidential election

The 1976 USA presidential election witnessed renewed criticisms of détente. The Democrats, who hoped to take back the White House, and a few Republicans, criticised détente for the following reasons:

- They argued that the Helsinki Accords were largely meaningless, as Eastern European countries were refusing to honour the sections of the agreement dealing with human rights. They pointed to the KGB's suppression of Yuri Orlov's Helsinki monitoring group in 1976. The group was closed down after it exposed non-compliance with the Helsinki Accords.

- Democrats argued that Kissinger's realpolitik had failed to gain the USA supremacy in the Cold War, as the SALT I Treaty allowed the USSR to retain a bigger nuclear arsenal than the USA.

## Essential notes

'Appeasement' means making concessions to avoid conflict. It was often applied to British policy in the 1930s towards Germany and was thereafter associated with weakness and failure.

Gerald Ford and Jimmy Carter debate national policy during the 1976 US presidential election

- The academic Richard Pipes argued that détente was being undermined by the Soviet Union, as it was arming nationalists to fight against US interests in the Third World.

Détente became so unpopular that Gerald Ford's advisors told him not to refer to the policy during the 1976 election.

## Critics of détente in the USSR

### Early critics of détente

In the Soviet Union too, there were concerns about pursuing a policy of détente. As early as 1969, Pytor Shelest, a member of the *Politburo*, criticised the policy on the basis that the US was engaged in the Vietnam War – a war with a communist nation. Tensions over the Vietnam War almost led to the cancellation of the Moscow Summit of 1972, as it coincided with a massive escalation of the war in Vietnam.

Other critics within the *Politburo*, such as Gennady Voronov, Alexsandr Shelepin and Nikolai Podgorny, were concerned about the more general implications of détente. Essentially, they argued that détente was an implicit acceptance of a bipolar world. By this, they meant that détente did nothing to challenge US dominance in the West. In this sense, détente would do nothing to advance the USSR's goal of spreading communism.

Events in the Middle East also led to criticism of détente within the Soviet government. The USSR had intelligence concerning the Middle East War, which it refused to share with the USA. As a result, the USA excluded the USSR from peace negotiations in the aftermath of the war. This damaged superpower relations and increased pressure on Brezhnev from within the *Politburo* to take a harder line against the USA.

### Criticisms after Nixon's fall

The Russian commitment to détente also weakened following 1974:

- Nixon's fall from power raised questions about the stability of the US government and the possibility of a long-term agreement between the two superpowers. Ford, who became President after Watergate, appointed new advisors such as Donald Rumsfeld, who were more committed to strengthening the position of the US than to détente. This change of team alarmed Soviet leaders because they could no longer count on US commitment to détente.

- The Soviet government was concerned that the USA was still committed to fighting the Cold War indirectly, by supporting anti-communist governments in the Third World, such as the Chilean government.

In spite of Soviet concerns, Brezhnev remained committed to détente, mentioning it favourably in his speech to the 1976 Party Congress.

**Examiners' notes**

Section A questions can be set on peaceful co-existence and on détente. The two periods are similar, and therefore easily confused. Make sure you have a clear idea of the differences between peaceful co-existence and détente in order to avoid confusing the two in the exam.

**Essential notes**

Republican Gerald Ford became President in 1974 after Richard Nixon was forced from office following the Watergate Scandal.

## Détente in decline

### Détente under Carter

Jimmy Carter became President in 1977. On taking office, Carter faced two major problems of foreign policy:

- SALT I was an interim agreement, and talks for SALT II, the final agreement between the superpowers, were progressing slowly.

- Détente was extremely unpopular with the American public, who viewed it as an amoral policy, which had effectively allowed Soviet influence to grow unchallenged.

### SALT II

In 1974, the USA and the USSR agreed on the 'Vladivostok Framework'. Each superpower would be allowed an 'equal ceiling' of 2400 missiles and bombers. However, there were technical difficulties about the classification of new technologies, including American Cruise Missiles and Russian 'Backfire Bombers'. The SALT II negotiations were unable to decide whether these new technologies counted as missiles or bombers, so a final agreement was impossible.

Further setbacks emerged when Carter took office. He effectively rejected the Vladivostok Framework, replacing the entire US negotiating team and demanding much lower ceilings. A year later, Carter further jeopardised talks by announcing a new nuclear project, the USA's largest government-funded construction project of all time, comprising 200 new missiles and 23 new silos, joined by underground railways. Finally, Carter agreed to upgrade America's nuclear deterrent by investing in the Trident II submarine.

Carter eventually backed down on his demand for lower ceilings and the USA and the USSR signed the SALT II Treaty in June 1979.

SALT II was significant because it exposed tensions in the US government between a minority who were committed to détente, and the majority who wanted the USA to take a tougher stance against the USSR.

### The Soviet invasion of Afghanistan

On December 24 1979, the USSR sent 50 000 Soviet troops to Kabul, the capital of Afghanistan. The Soviet invasion spelled the end of détente.

In essence, the Soviet Union were acting defensively to protect the Communist regime in Afghanistan, which was under threat from Islamic fundamentalists. As far as Brezhnev was concerned, the invasion was designed to retain the USSR's only foothold in the Middle East rather than as the first step to expanding its influence in that region.

The American government interpreted the Soviet invasion very differently and thus the invasion shifted the balance of power in Carter's government.

### Essential notes

Carter's approach to the Cold War has often been described as 'schizophrenic', meaning that it can appear contradictory. On the one hand, he wanted to do more than Nixon and Ford to reduce nuclear stockpiles, and on the other, he wanted to appear tougher than Nixon or Ford in his dealings with Brezhnev.

Prior to the invasion, the Carter administration was divided on the merits of détente. Cyrus Vance, Carter's Secretary of State, was in favour of maintaining détente in the interests of world peace.

Zbigniew Brzezinski, Carter's National Security Advisor, was in favour of a more assertive American policy designed to expose and exploit the weaknesses of the USSR.

The invasion shifted the balance of power away from the supporters of détente and towards the supporters of confrontation. The Soviet invasion went beyond the 'Brezhnev Doctrine', indicating to Brzezinski that the USSR was pursuing an aggressive policy of expansion in the oil-rich Middle East.

## The USA's response to the invasion of Afghanistan

Carter responded to the Soviet invasion by demanding the withdrawal of Soviet troops. He argued that Afghanistan should remain non-aligned, part of neither sphere of influence. In February 1980, Carter started a grain embargo against the USSR and secretly sent military aid to the Mujahedeen, the Islamic fundamentalists who were committed to forcing the USSR out of Afghanistan. Carter's goal was to make the war as costly as possible for the USSR. In this sense, he was keen to exploit the growing imbalance of economic power between the superpowers.

However, Carter's demand for Soviet withdrawal failed to force the Soviet Union to pull out of Afghanistan. This made Carter seem weak.

## The significance of the invasion of Afghanistan

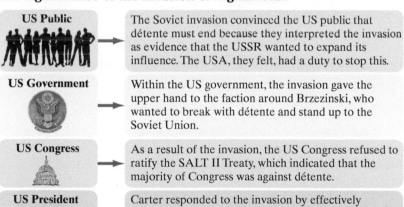

| | |
|---|---|
| **US Public** | The Soviet invasion convinced the US public that détente must end because they interpreted the invasion as evidence that the USSR wanted to expand its influence. The USA, they felt, had a duty to stop this. |
| **US Government** | Within the US government, the invasion gave the upper hand to the faction around Brzezinski, who wanted to break with détente and stand up to the Soviet Union. |
| **US Congress** | As a result of the invasion, the US Congress refused to ratify the SALT II Treaty, which indicated that the majority of Congress was against détente. |
| **US President** | Carter responded to the invasion by effectively abandoning détente. This was indicated in a series of leaked Presidential directives in which the US government set out its plans for winning and surviving a nuclear war. Carter's directives signalled the end of détente and the cooling of relations with the USSR. |

## Essential notes

'Rolling back the state' was Margaret Thatcher's term for reducing the extent to which the government interfered in the economy. Thatcher and Reagan both agreed that, following the Second World War, the state had become too active and sought to redress the balance between the state and private enterprise. This is related to their criticisms of the USSR. Essentially, both believed that the defining feature of communism was state interference. Therefore, by 'rolling back the state' at home, they were combating communist aspects of Western culture.

# Thatcher and Reagan: the end of détente, 1979–81

## Election victories

Margaret Thatcher was elected Prime Minister of Britain in 1979. Ronald Reagan was elected President of the US a year later. Both leaders represented a new kind of conservatism that was determined to revitalise capitalism at home and stand up to communism abroad.

## 'The Thatcher–Reagan love-in'

The love-in is so-named because 'Thatcherism' and 'Reaganomics' were similar in many ways. Both leaders were committed to the same things, as shown in the diagram.

**Encouraging free enterprise by 'rolling back the state'**
Thatcher and Reagan believed that government spending and high taxes dominated the economies of Britain and the USA. They believed that high taxes and big government were damaging to private enterprise.

**Defence spending**
Both leaders were committed to expanding government spending on defence. Specifically, both were dedicated to a new generation of nuclear missiles called *Trident*. This presented problems for the USSR. The growing imbalance of economic power meant that the USSR could not afford to keep pace with the defence spending of the West.

**'Thatcherism' and 'Reaganomics' were similar in many ways, as both leaders were committed to the same things.**

**Standing up to the 'Evil Empire'**
Reagan and Thatcher had a similar view of the USSR. They both believed that communism was a moral evil that the West had a duty to oppose.

This new brand of conservatism was significant as it consolidated the move away from détente that had been initiated by Carter. Both Thatcher and Reagan had an ideological view of foreign policy that stressed the need to strengthen capitalism and undermine communism.

## Reagan in power

As the leader of one of the world's superpowers, President Reagan was the more important partner in the Thatcher–Reagan axis. Reagan's foreign policy was designed to assert US strength and weaken the position of the USSR. He set out to do this in the following ways:

- Reagan restricted trade with the USSR to deny them access to superior Western technology.

- He committed the US government to a massive defence project – the Strategic Defence Initiative (SDI). This initiative was popularly known as 'Star Wars', as it consisted of a space-based nuclear shield. Reagan proposed a fleet of US satellites armed with lasers that would shoot down Soviet missiles before they could harm the USA.

- Reagan increased support for anti-Soviet regimes and organisations in the Third World.

- He used confrontational rhetoric, including the phrase 'Evil Empire' to describe the USSR.

However, Reagan did not seek war. In fact, in an attempt to reach out to Soviet leaders, he lifted the grain embargo that Carter had imposed in 1980.

### The significance of Reagan's policies

'Star Wars' was particularly significant. The new policy worried Soviet leaders for two reasons:

- Soviet leaders knew that they would be unable to compete with 'Star Wars'. During the 1970s, the USA had produced sophisticated computer technology, which far surpassed anything that was available in the Soviet Union. This technology would form the basis of 'Star Wars'. The economic problems in the Eastern Bloc and renewed growth in the West had accentuated the imbalance of economic power in favour of the West. Soviet leaders knew that they could not match the USA's spending commitment to 'Star Wars'.

- 'Star Wars' implied that Reagan was contemplating a 'winnable nuclear war'. A space-based missile shield could, in theory, counter a Soviet nuclear attack, allowing the USA to survive a nuclear war unscathed. Therefore, the USSR's nuclear arsenal would no longer deter a US nuclear strike.

Reagan's new confrontational style was significant because it increased tension between the governments of the superpowers. Andrei Gromyko, a senior member of the Russian government, noted an increased 'chill' in superpower relations from Reagan's inauguration as President in January 1981. Indeed, Reagan made inflammatory off-the-cuff remarks about the possibility of 'a limited nuclear war in Europe', which caused great concern to communist leaders. The diagram below shows the US decline of commitment to détente:

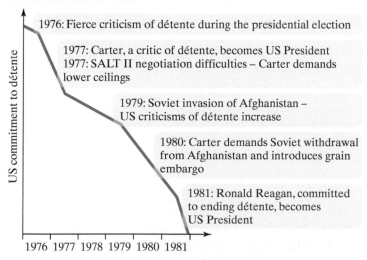

### Examiners' notes

When planning an answer to a Section A question, it is important to ensure that the approach is thematic rather than chronological. For example, when writing an essay on the reasons for the failure of détente, you could consider the following themes:

- the Soviet invasion of Afghanistan

- the role of the presidents

- the role of critics of détente in the US

- the role of critics of détente in the USSR

- the economic realities of détente.

### Essential notes

US Presidential elections happen in November, but the winning candidate does not take office until January of the next year. This means that the year in which a president is elected is not the same as the year in which he or she takes office. For example, Reagan was elected in 1980, but only took office in 1981.

## Ronald Reagan and US foreign policy in the 1980s

### Reagan's foreign policy objectives

On becoming President in 1981, Ronald Reagan rejected détente as a 'communist trick'. As noted on page 74, Reagan had the following foreign policy objectives:

US foreign policy should be used to weaken the position of the USSR.

Trade with the USSR should be restricted to deny the USSR access to superior Western technology.

US defence spending should increase because the US economy is stronger than the Soviet economy – the USSR will never be able to match it.

| Objective | Relevant policy |
| --- | --- |
| To weaken the position of the USSR | The Reagan Doctrine Changing diplomacy SDI |
| To restrict trade with the USSR | Trade restrictions |
| To increase US defence spending | SDI |

### Reagan's foreign policy in practice

#### The Reagan Doctrine

Reagan hoped to weaken the USSR by providing US support to anti-communist 'freedom fighters' around the world. This commitment became known as the Reagan Doctrine. A key example of the Reagan Doctrine in action was US support for the Mujahideen in the battle against the Soviet occupation of Afghanistan.

#### Changing diplomacy

During Reagan's first term as president, the most important change was the way in which US foreign policy was presented to the US public, and the world at large.

Reagan believed that previous presidents had failed to convince the US public of the need for an ongoing battle against communism. He believed that support for the US position in the Cold War had dropped due to US failure in Vietnam. For Reagan, the Cold War was a moral mission and he felt that the US public should stand behind their government. Reagan changed the government's approach through increasingly hard-line rhetoric (public-speaking). The best example was his speech in 1983, in which he described the USSR as an 'Evil Empire'.

In addition, Reagan made a series of public statements about the US relationship with the world. For example, he publically discussed the USA's revised policy on nuclear war against the USSR. He argued that the USA was prepared for a 'limited nuclear war in Europe'. This persuaded senior Soviet military leaders that the USA was considering options for a first strike in a nuclear war.

At home and abroad, Reagan's diplomacy weakened the Soviet position. In the USA, Reagan's hard-line rhetoric won domestic support for increased spending on defence, ensuring that the USA had a superior position in the arms race. In addition, Reagan's diplomacy gave the initiative in the Cold War to the West.

## Trade restrictions

Reagan introduced a series of trade restrictions to reduce the USSR's ability to buy Western technology and energy:

- In December 1981, Reagan restricted Soviet access to US-developed energy exploration technology.

- In June 1982, Reagan restricted Soviet access to US oil and gas and related technical data.

## SDI 'Star Wars'

In 1984, Reagan initiated the SDI (Strategic Defence Initiative). Essentially, Reagan was prepared to negotiate arms reduction treaties with the USSR but he wanted to negotiate from a position of strength. The 'Star Wars' project put the US in a position of strength because it had the potential to provide a shield against Soviet missiles, and the USSR could not match the space or computer technology that was necessary to create the shield.

## Reagan's foreign policy and the end of the Cold War

Reagan's foreign policy was not intended to end the Cold War, but rather to weaken the USSR. In fact, Reagan's policy was so successful at weakening the USSR that it played a major role in ending the Cold War.

| Policy initiative | Significance for the end of the Cold War |
|---|---|
| The Reagan Doctrine | The Reagan Doctrine decreased the financial resources and the political legitimacy of the USSR. For example, support for the Mujahideen prolonged the war in Afghanistan. This proved costly for the Soviets in three ways: <br><br> 1. Financially, the war drained Soviet resources. <br><br> 2. The war was unpopular among the Russian people, and so weakened support for the Soviet government. <br><br> 3. The war was unpopular internationally, and so weakened support for the USSR among the international community. |
| Changing diplomacy and SDI | Reagan's proactive approach to the Cold War forced the USSR to consider nuclear war as a real threat. However, Soviet leaders realised that the USA had a clear military advantage. Therefore, elements in the Soviet government began to consider a negotiated end to the arms race. |
| Trade restrictions | Limiting Soviet access to America's energy and technology exposed the weaknesses of the Soviet economy in the minds of Soviet leaders. In this sense, the restrictions led to a crisis of confidence at the top of the Soviet government. |

## Source 1
(From Norman A. Graebner, Richard Dean Burns, Joseph M. Siracusa, *Reagan, Bush, Gorbachev: revisiting the end of the Cold War*, published by Greenwood Publishing 2008)

Citizens and historians have long questioned – after more than forty years of Cold War rivalry – what was responsible for its end? Among the causes most often put forward has been that of the technical and economic challenges posed by the Reagan administration's extensive arms build up. It was, and is, argued that Soviet Union's economic malaise, caused by its efforts to match US military spending, prompted Kremlin leaders to surrender.

**Essential notes**

Energy exploration technology refers to technology that has been designed to find new reserves of oil, coal and gas.

**Examiners' notes**

In Source 1 the authors summarise the interpretation of Paul Johnson before offering their critique. When using a source of this kind, it is important to distinguish between the views of the author and those of the historian being referenced.

**Economic problems**
- The standard of living in Poland was low and declining.
- From 1980, food shortages became serious.
- Due to poor economic growth, the government could no longer afford to subsidise the price of food, so prices continued to rise.

**Political unrest**
On May 3 1980, Polish people took to the streets in large-scale marches to complain about the price increases. In August, an illegal trade union, 'Solidarity', organised the Gdansk Strike.

**Government response**
Initially, the government compromised, allowing wage increases and recognising Solidarity. However, Solidarity demanded greater political liberalisation and the introduction of democracy. As a result, in December 1981, the Polish Premier introduced martial law, arresting 200000 people. The revolt was crushed and without organised opposition, the government was able to increase the price of goods even more.

## Essential notes

Traditionally, communist governments had subsidised the cost of goods to ensure that they remained affordable. When subsidies could no longer be provided, the Polish government had to increase the price of essential products.

## Weakening Soviet control over Eastern Europe

### The USSR and Eastern Europe

During the 1980s the USSR lost control over Eastern Europe. The process began in Poland in 1980. An unpopular war in Afghanistan, international pressure, and Soviet economic problems meant that Brezhnev found it hard to assert Soviet control over Poland.

### Poland, 1980–81

Economic problems in Poland led to an escalation of protest and repression, as shown in the diagram.

The Polish crisis was significant because it reflected the USSR's weakening control over Eastern Europe:

- The Soviet invasion of Afghanistan created international outrage, so Brezhnev felt unable to send Soviet troops to end the unrest in Poland. This implied a rejection of the Brezhnev Doctrine.

- Brezhnev was unwilling to impose economic sanctions on Poland. The Soviet economy was in a period of decline, which made trade with Poland extremely valuable to the USSR.

Brezhnev had not lost control of Polish politics. It was at his urging that the Polish Premier imposed martial law. As a result, political peace and communist control was maintained until the mid-1980s.

### The role of Pope John Paul II

Pope John Paul II played an important role in the Polish crisis. In 1979, he became the first Polish Pope to be elected, which inspired great nationalism in the Polish nation. Though the Roman Catholic Church was already an important part of Polish life, it now became a focal point for anti-communism feeling. And the Pope's visit to Poland in 1979 helped the growth of anti-communist nationalism. Indeed, during the Gdansk strike, a picture of the Pope was placed on the gates of the Gdansk shipyard. During the 1980s, the Pope continually signalled his support for the Solidarity Union and for democratic reform in Poland. The Pope's role was important because his support gave the protestors greater authority in their fight against communism.

### Instability in the USSR, 1980–84

During 1980–84, the USSR was fighting an unpopular war in Afghanistan and facing unrest in the Eastern Bloc, particularly Poland. During this period, the Soviet government was unable to offer effective leadership because its rulers had chronic health problems. The weakness at the top of Soviet government meant that its leaders were unable to address the mounting political and economic problems that faced the USSR.

### Gorbachev and the 'New Thinking'

In March 1985, Mikhail Gorbachev became Soviet Premier. He was willing to admit that the USSR faced real problems and that he had to consider radical solutions.

| Problem facing the USSR | Gorbachev's solution |
|---|---|
| Economic decline | *Perestroika* (restructuring). Workers and managers should be given greater power to make economic decisions. This would remove power from the Soviet central planning authority – *Gosplan*. |
| Public loss of faith in communism | *Glasnost* (openness). Corrupt and lazy members of the Communist Party should be removed. The government should admit past mistakes, and reduce censorship of the press. |
| The burden of military spending | Gorbachev argued that spending on nuclear weapons did nothing to guarantee the security of the Soviet Union, and he sought arms reduction talks with the USA to ensure security through dialogue rather than through mutually assured destruction (MAD). |

## Essential notes

Between 1980 and 1982, Brezhnev was very ill and therefore unable fulfil his role as Soviet Premier. In November 1982, Brezhnev died and was replaced by Yuri Andropov. Andropov himself had health problems and died in February 1984. He was replaced by Konstantin Chernenko, who was also ill, and died in March 1985.

## Nuclear diplomacy

Gorbachev sought to reduce the nuclear arsenals on both sides of the Cold War. At a series of summits, Gorbachev and Reagan worked together to bring about the first arms reduction treaty of the Cold War.

| Summit | Proposals and agreement |
|---|---|
| Geneva Summit (November 1985) | Gorbachev proposed a 50 per cent cut in the total number of US and Soviet nuclear weapons if the USA would stop developing SDI. Reagan refused to give up SDI and no agreement was reached. |
| Reykjavik Summit (September 1986) | Gorbachev proposed to eliminate all nuclear weapons by the year 2000 if the USA would stop developing SDI. Reagan refused to give up SDI and no agreement was reached. |
| Intermediate-range Nuclear Forces (INF) Treaty (December 1987) | Gorbachev dropped his insistence that SDI should be discontinued. As a result, the USA and the USSR agreed that all intermediate-range nuclear missiles should be scrapped. This meant a reduction of 1750 Soviet missiles and 850 US missiles. |

## The role of Margaret Thatcher

Margaret Thatcher helped Reagan in his mission to challenge the Soviet Union, in that she consistently supported his foreign policy, allowed US nuclear weapons to be stationed on British soil (considerably nearer to Russia than the USA), and demonstrated her opposition to communism by investing in a new generation of British nuclear weapons.

Thatcher also helped to bridge the gap between Reagan and Gorbachev. Thatcher's good opinion of Gorbachev played a role in Reagan's approach to the new Soviet leader.

## Essential notes

The INF Treaty led to a reduction in the size of the US and Soviet nuclear arsenal. Therefore, it was known as an arms reduction treaty, in contrast to the SALT agreements, which merely limited the growth of nuclear arsenals.

### The end of the Cold War

In the period 1987–9, events in the Soviet Union and Eastern Europe moved at a remarkable pace. By 9 November 1990, the Berlin Wall had come down and the Cold War was effectively over. The pace of communism's collapse in Eastern Europe and the end of the Cold War surprised politicians and experts alike.

### Gorbachev's final reforms

During the final years of the 1980s, Gorbachev extended *perestroika*, introducing greater decentralisation in the economy and elements of choice in Soviet elections. The most significant change in policy was the official abandonment of the Brezhnev Doctrine during 1988–9. This led to the collapse of communism across Eastern Europe.

### The fall of the Berlin Wall

Poland and Hungary were the first countries to test the end of the Brezhnev Doctrine. The fall of communism in Hungary was particularly noteworthy. Following the fall of communism, Hungary opened its borders with the West, allowing East German citizens to travel via Hungary to West Germany. In September alone, 10 000 East Germans made the trip to the West. Consequently, the East German government agreed to open Checkpoint Charlie. Berliners from East and West flocked to the Wall and began to tear it down. The fall of the Berlin Wall became symbolic of the end of the Cold War, the end of a divided Europe, and victory for 'people power'.

**East Germany**
The fall of the Berlin Wall in 1989 brought East Germany's communist government to an end. Elections were held in March 1990, and Germany was reunited in October of that year.

**Poland**
Following a wave of strikes in 1988, the communist government was forced to negotiate with Solidarity. By September 1989, Poland had a non-communist Prime Minister. Significantly, after the end of the Brezhnev Doctrine, Gorbachev did nothing to challenge the fall of communism in Poland, which prompted change across Eastern Europe.

**Czechoslovakia**
The Velvet Revolution of November 1989 handed power peacefully to a democratically elected government.

**Romania**
The Romanian dictator, Nicolae Ceausescu, was overthrown on Christmas Day 1989.

**Hungary**
In January 1989, the Communist Party announced multi-party elections with the approval of Gorbachev. The first democratic government was elected in April 1990.

**Bulgaria**
Free elections were held in June 1990.

**Yugoslavia**
During 1990, nationalist groups in Yugoslavia's six major regions won democratic elections, leading to the break-up of Yugoslavia.

**Albania**
Free elections were held in March 1991.

### The fall of communism in Eastern Europe

Between 1989 and 1991, communism regimes were replaced by democratically elected governments throughout the Eastern Bloc, as shown in the following diagram.

### Gorbachev's role in the collapse of communism

Initially, Gorbachev played a permissive role by abandoning the Brezhnev Doctrine and announcing that each communist country should 'find its own path to socialism'. By saying this, he implied that Eastern European countries should continue to work towards communism, but should be free of Russian influence.

However, once freed of Russian influence, communism quickly collapsed. During 1989, Gorbachev became more radical, actively encouraging communist governments to negotiate with opposition groups. He even advised the East German government to open its border with the West.

### The US role in the collapse of communism

During 1989, new US President George Bush welcomed the changes in Eastern Europe. He was praised for his tact and for not gloating as the Soviet Union, the USA's long-standing enemy, began to collapse.

### The fall of the USSR

Neither Gorbachev nor Bush actively tried to break up the USSR. Nonetheless, nationalist movements in the Soviet republics followed the example of countries from the Eastern Bloc and began to move towards independence. To prevent the break-up of the USSR, Communist hard-liners staged a coup in August 1991, temporarily removing Gorbachev from power. The coup failed and so did Gorbachev's attempt to hold the USSR together. Gorbachev resigned on 25 December 1991, and the USSR ceased to exist a day later.

> **Source 2**
> (From Robert J. McMahon, *The Cold War: A Very Short Introduction*, published by Oxford University Press 2003)
>
> The accession, in March 1985, of Mikhail Gorbachev to the position of general secretary of the Soviet Communist Party, stands as the most critical turning point in the Cold War's final phase – the one factor, above all others, that hastened the end of the Cold War and the radical transformation in Soviet-American relations ... Through a series of wholly unexpected, often unilateral, overturea and concessions, he succeeded in changing the entire tenor of Soviet–US relations.

**Examiners' notes**

Telling the story of the break-up of the Eastern Bloc is unlikely to get you into the highest levels of the mark scheme. It is better to refer to specific examples that illustrate clear points, rather than listing the order in which countries abandoned communism.

**Examiners' notes**

Some of the content for the second controversy overlaps with content you have looked at during your study of détente. It is acceptable to draw on this knowledge when answering a Section B question about the end of the Cold War. However, remember that the Section A question will never require knowledge of the period after 1981.

**Examiners' notes**

Source 2 states clearly that Gorbachev played a major role in bringing about the end of the Cold War. Nonetheless, it does not necessarily exclude the possibility that Reagan also played a vital role. When dealing with sources in the exam, do not assume that different interpretations are contradictory interpretations.

## Examiners' notes

Here you need to:

- understand the key features of the pro-Reagan triumphalist interpretation of the end of the Cold War (be aware that Reagan shifted to a more accommodating approach after Gorbachev became Soviet leader)
- identify the strengths and weaknesses of this perspective to help with the evaluation
- assess the relative importance of Margaret Thatcher and Pope John Paul II in bringing the Cold War to an end (consider the contribution made by these two important individuals).

# The role of personalities: Reagan, Thatcher and Pope John Paul II

## Reagan and the triumphalists

The triumphalist argument maintains that Reagan's hard-line approach to the USSR in the early 1980s imposed enormous economic and military pressure on the Soviet Union. As a result, the USSR could no longer compete with US defence spending and thus had to abandon the arms race and the Cold War. According to this interpretation, Reagan's successful anti-communist policies included:

- a 53 per cent increase in the US defence budget (October 1981), designed, in part, to fund the B1 bomber, neutron bomb and stealth aircraft programmes, US navy expansion and the deployment of MX missiles
- the announcement of the Strategic Defence Initiative (SDI) in March 1983
- uncompromising anti-Soviet, 'Evil Empire' rhetoric
- implementation of the Reagan Doctrine including US military and financial measures to combat communism in Nicaragua, El Salvador, Grenada and Afghanistan
- deployment of cruise and Pershing II missiles in Europe.

### Criticism of the triumphalist interpretation

Numerous historians and some members of the Reagan administration (including former Secretary of State, George Schultz), have argued that the triumphalist explanation of the end of the Cold War oversimplifies a complex historical process and exaggerates the impact of Reagan's hard-line approach. The main criticisms included:

- From 1982 to 1984, Reagan's uncompromising stance failed to extract concessions from Soviet leader Andropov. Indeed, the USA's confrontational strategy merely prolonged the Cold War by hardening Soviet resistance.
- Reagan's offer to share SDI technology with the USSR contradicts the argument that the USA aimed to undermine the Soviet Union economically.
- Soviet scientists concluded that the SDI was impractical, so it imposed limited pressure on the USSR.
- Reagan and Bush's policy of constructive engagement with Gorbachev after 1985 produced much more significant results (for example, the 1987 INF Treaty and the 1991 START Treaty).
- The triumphalist view underestimates the role of other factors in ending the Cold War, such as Gorbachev's 'New Thinking', the long-standing internal Soviet problems and growing popular discontent in Eastern Europe.

## Margaret Thatcher

Many 'triumphalist' historians assert that the British Prime Minister, Margaret Thatcher, played an important, if secondary, role in bringing the Cold War to an end. As has been noted, Thatcher supported Reagan's anti-Soviet strategy of 'militarised counter-revolution', and later claimed that this US policy was the reason the West 'won'.

### *Thatcher's support for Reagan's policies*

Thatcher reinforced Reagan's anti-communist rhetoric. In October 1982, for example, she remarked that the Soviets' 'pitiless ideology only survives because it is maintained by force'. From November 1983, Thatcher also permitted the USA to deploy cruise missiles in Britain, a key feature of Reagan's plan to pressure the USSR. Furthermore, Thatcher acted as Reagan's unofficial envoy by promoting US policy to other West European governments.

The 'Iron Lady' (as the Soviet press had named her) also pursued some less confrontational policies, which contradicted her 'Cold War warrior' image. In 1984, for example, she invited Gorbachev to London for talks before he came to power. She established a good working relationship with him, famously remarking, 'This is a man I can do business with'. She then urged Reagan to start a dialogue with Gorbachev. Thatcher later endorsed *perestroika* and acted as an effective diplomatic link between Gorbachev and Presidents Reagan and Bush.

## Pope John Paul II

The Polish Pope, John Paul II, also made a significant contribution to ending the Cold War, by inspiring Catholics in Eastern Europe and providing moral support for the Polish trade union Solidarity:

- Pope John Paul II's visits to Poland in 1979, 1983 and 1987 were enormously popular (some 12 million Poles saw the Pope on his 1979 tour). The visits clearly indicated that Catholicism rather than communism commanded public loyalty. Historian Michael Burleigh has described the Pope's 1979 Polish visit as a 'gigantic anti-communist plebiscite'.

- The Pope rejected the Polish regime's claim that the Catholic Church had no social role.

- In January 1981, Lech Walesa, the Solidarity leader and a devout Catholic, was blessed by the Pope in Rome. The significance of the event was obvious.

- The Pope's speeches, for example, 'Do not be afraid' in 1979, encouraged anti-communists and made the Polish people more self-confident.

Nevertheless, the Pope's influence had limits. Catholicism attracted wide support in Poland and the Baltic states, but elsewhere in Eastern Europe – where it had to compete with Protestantism, the Orthodox Church and secularism – it had less impact.

**Essential notes**

Margaret Thatcher (1925–) served as the British Conservative Prime Minister from 1979 to 1990. As a staunch anti-communist and advocate of free-market economics, she believed strongly in what she called Britain's 'enduring alliance' with the USA.

**Essential notes**

A conservative Catholic, John Paul II criticised human rights abuses in the Eastern Bloc, took a public stand against communism,.

**Essential notes**

The triumphalist interpretation is favoured by the political right to explain the West's victory in the Cold War.

### Examiners' notes

Here you need to:

- understand the key features of the pro-Gorbachev interpretation of the end of the Cold War (be aware of the connections between Gorbachev's domestic aims and his foreign policy objectives, as they are strongly linked)
- identify the strengths and weaknesses of this perspective (the pro-Gorbachev interpretation of the end of the Cold War is popular in the West so make sure you are familiar with, and can evaluate, criticisms of this approach).

## The role of personalities: Gorbachev

### The pro-Gorbachev view

Other historians stress Gorbachev's role in ending the Cold War. In their view, he was unwilling to perpetuate the Cold War stalemate and worked to create genuine East–West understanding by adopting new policies to build trust, reduce Cold War tensions and solve the USSR's economic problems.

### Source 3

(From Jeremy Isaacs and Taylor Downing, *Cold War*, published by Abacus 2008)

Gorbachev was a Soviet leader with a new line of thinking, who no longer fitted the mould of the past. Gorbachev, in countless speeches, stressed his commitment to arms reduction and his unwillingness to play the game of his predecessors. He argued that confrontation was simply not a stable basis for peace. Compromise, mutual trust, and co-operation would be the way forward. Fundamental structural changes were necessary to the Soviet system if it was to survive. The Soviet economy was desperately weak; it could no longer play the superpower role in supporting an ever-spiralling arms race. A stop had to be called, and Gorbachev called it.

According to this interpretation, Gorbachev contributed to the end of the Cold War in some significant ways, as listed in the following table.

| Gorbachev's key actions | |
| --- | --- |
| Gorbachev pursued arms reductions to lower the risk of nuclear war and ease the economic burden on the USSR. | In 1987, he negotiated the INF Treaty with the USA, which dismantled a whole class of intermediate-range nuclear missiles. |
| | In 1991, he concluded the START Agreement with the USA, which reduced overall nuclear arsenals by 30 per cent. |
| Gorbachev removed the ideological basis of the Cold War and promoted *glasnost* and *perestroika*. | His landmark UN speech (1988) abandoned the Brezhnev Doctrine, endorsed freedom of choice and dismissed Marxist-Leninism as irrelevant. |
| | He introduced *perestroika* reforms into the Soviet economy in 1986. |
| | He informed East European communist leaders that they would have to govern without Soviet support (April 1989). |
| | *Glasnost* gave the Soviet satellite countries the right to choose their own paths. |

### Examiners' notes

Section B questions require you to use the source material provided, to develop the analysis. One way is to recognise that a single source could offer more than one line of argument. For example, if you were answering the question, 'To what extent were Gorbachev's policies responsible for the end of the Cold War in the 1980s?', and were given Source 3, you would need to be aware that this extract provides material to develop the pro-Gorbachev viewpoint *and* the economic factors argument. You could then link the two.

| Gorbachev's key actions | |
|---|---|
| Gorbachev ended 'old style' Soviet aggression and expansionism. | He announced in 1988 that Soviet forces in Eastern Europe would be reduced by 500 000. |
| | He withdrew Soviet forces from Afghanistan by 1989. |
| | He ended Soviet financial support to Ethiopia, Vietnam, Cambodia, Nicaragua and Angola. |
| | He refused to suppress popular protests in Eastern Europe or prevent the liberalisation of the Soviet Bloc. |

## Criticism of the pro-Gorbachev interpretation

The pro-Gorbachev interpretation has been challenged on the grounds that it oversimplifies a complicated historical process, and exaggerates Gorbachev's personal impact.

Some of the main criticisms include:

- The complex and often unpredictable developments that ended the Cold War were beyond one leader's ability to control.
- The pro-Gorbachev view underestimates the constructive role played by Reagan from 1984 in seeking a better US–Soviet relationship.
- Gorbachev-centred explanations can underplay the broader structural factors that helped to end the Cold War such as Soviet economic problems and growing social discontent in the satellite states.
- Some Soviet commentators, for example, Sergei Akhromeyev and Georgi Kornienko, have argued that Gorbachev 'caved in' to the West due to pressure exerted on the Soviet Union by a US campaign of subversion.

## The 'role of key personalities' interpretation: an overall assessment

| Strengths | This focuses on the key individuals who made the major decisions or wielded significant influence during the years leading up to the end of the Cold War. |
|---|---|
| | This approach is particularly valuable in examining Soviet behaviour, bearing in mind Gorbachev's radically new approach to Cold War relations. |
| | It can also reveal the constraints and pressures under which the national leaders had to operate during the closing stages of the Cold War. |
| Weaknesses | Personality-based explanations may exaggerate the importance of a key individual in the events and developments that ended the Cold War. |
| | Such an approach may underestimate the relative importance of structural factors such as economic problems and social discontent. |

### Essential notes

The pro-Gorbachev explanation challenges the triumphalist viewpoint by emphasising that the Soviet leader was the key political actor in the final phase of the Cold War. This interpretation maintains:

- Gorbachev was the first leader of the USSR who abandoned the traditional Soviet approach to Cold War relations in favour of international co-operation and compromise.
- He had the ability to build bonds of trust with key Western leaders, notably Reagan, Thatcher and Bush.
- His 'New Thinking', based on *perestroika*, *glasnost* and arms reductions, transformed East–West relations after 1985.
- Gorbachev's initiatives encouraged political reform in Eastern Europe and led to the dissolution of the Soviet Bloc.

Historians who partly or wholly endorse the pro-Gorbachev viewpoint include Robert J. McMahon, Archie Brown, Raymond L. Garthoff, Jeremy Isaacs and Taylor Downing.

## The impact of economic factors

### The economic burden of the Cold War

East–West conflict imposed enormous economic burdens on the superpowers, particularly the Soviet Union. As a result, many historians have argued that economic factors played a major role in undermining the capacity of the USSR to continue the Cold War:

### Source 4

(From David S. Painter *The Cold War: An International History*, published by Routledge 1999)

The inability of the Soviet Union's economy to compete with the West restricted its citizens' standard of living, threatened its national security, and ultimately eroded the legitimacy of the communist system … Military competition with the United States and the PRC forced the Soviets to devote a much larger share of their smaller gross national product to defence, and siphoned off resources needed for economic modernisation and development. The diversion of investment away from productive sectors and consumer goods ultimately undermined the Soviet Union's willingness and ability to compete with the United States and to maintain its empire. Economic growth in the Soviet bloc, which had risen in the late 1940s and 1950s, began to slow in the early 1970s and never recovered.

### The stagnant Soviet economy

Almost until the very end of the Cold War, Soviet propaganda claimed that the USSR was on the verge of overtaking the developed capitalist economies of the West. In 1959, Khrushchev famously bragged that the Soviet Union would 'bury' the USA economically and, eight years later, the USSR predicted that industrial production would increase by about 50 per cent. In addition, *Novosti*, the Soviet press agency, produced much publicity material in the 1980s (for Western consumption), which portrayed the USSR as an increasingly dominant, and economically developed, superpower. The reality, however, was very different (as the table on the next page illustrates). From the early 1970s the Soviet economy was actually stagnating, due to:

- the enormous costs of the arms race

- the unrealistic production targets of the Five-Year Plans

- inefficient central planning methods

- inadequate infrastructure and technology

- corruption within the Soviet elite – *nomenklatura* (see page 92).

| Soviet economic performance | | |
|---|---|---|
| Annual growth rate for industrial output | 5.25 per cent (1967) | 2 per cent (1980) |
| Average annual increase in national income | 3.4 per cent (1961–1975) | 1.1 per cent (1976–1990) |
| Annual growth rate for agricultural output | 3.7 per cent (1970) | 0.8 per cent (1980) |

**Essential notes**

GDP, or Gross Domestic Product, is the monetary value of all that is produced (goods and services) in a country in one year.

Furthermore, the USSR's growing reliance, from the early 1970s, on the export of oil and gas was hit by a downturn in world energy prices during the following decade.

Oil accounted for 15.6 per cent of Soviet exports in 1970 but by 1984 this had risen to over 54 per cent. West Siberian oil production increased from 31 million tons in 1970 to 312 million tons in 1980. Over the same period, natural gas output rose from 9.5 million to 156 million cubic metres. However, between 1980–81 and 1988 the real value of crude oil and natural gas dropped by 90 per cent and 50 per cent, respectively.

### Technological backwardness

Technologically, the Soviet Union lagged far behind the USA in most respects, and the USA took steps to maintain this advantage. The West imposed a co-ordinated technology embargo on the Soviet Bloc in 1950, which was not lifted during the détente years. Indeed, in 1974 the USA banned the sale of advanced computers to the USSR and its allies.

Moreover, features of the Soviet system discouraged technological progress. The police limited the use of photocopiers and personal computers (PCs) because of the threat they posed to the state's absolute control. By the early 1980s, there were only 50 000 PCs in the USSR, compared to 30 million in the USA, and these PCs were years behind American models. The Soviet government's mainframe computers were also outdated in comparison. By the 1980s, technological inferiority in key areas (such as computers, microelectronics and telecommunications) placed the USSR at a significant military disadvantage.

The 'economic factors' interpretation maintains that:

- The Cold War placed huge economic strains on both superpowers, but particularly the Soviet Union.
- By the 1980s, the USSR faced mounting economic problems due to:
    - the inefficiency of centralised state economic planning
    - the financial burden of maintaining the Soviet empire
    - the escalating costs of the nuclear arms race.
- These serious economic difficulties prompted Gorbachev's 'New Thinking' and compelled the Soviet Union to opt out of an unsustainable Cold War.

Historians who have emphasised the 'economic factors' viewpoint include Jeremy Isaacs, Taylor Downing and David S. Painter.

**Essential notes**

Reasons the USA was in a stronger economic position than the Soviets:

- The Soviet economy was about 50 per cent smaller.
- The US economy was more productive.
- Technologically, most sectors of the Soviet economy were far behind the USA.
- Unlike the USA, the Soviet economy manufactured poor-quality products and suffered shortages of essential materials.

Continued on the next two pages

## Examiners' notes

Section B questions require you to integrate your own knowledge with the source material provided to develop the argument. For example, if you were answering the question 'To what extent were mounting Soviet economic problems responsible for the end of the Cold War in the 1980s?', and were given Source 4 to help you, you would need to provide your own evidence to support the following points from the extract:

- A large proportion of Soviet GDP went to defence.
- Other sectors of the Soviet economy were starved of investment.
- There was little or no economic growth.

## A costly empire

The Soviet empire also acted as an economic drain on the USSR. In theory, the Soviet Union should have been an affluent superpower, bearing in mind the huge reserves of natural resources (including oil, gas and metal ores) that were located in Siberia. In practice, however, favourable trading arrangements with its socialist allies ensured that the USSR saw relatively little of this potential wealth. Soviet energy and raw materials were sold to these states at very low prices in return for low-grade industrial or consumer goods. Between 1981 and 1986, for example, the USSR provided Cuba and Vietnam with $4 billion and $6 billion, respectively, in aid and oil subsidies. The Warsaw Pact countries also received a yearly subsidy of some $3 billion due to cheap oil sent from the Soviet Union.

This relationship encouraged relative economic backwardness in the Soviet Bloc and contributed to low living standards in the USSR.

## The arms race

Although the arms race imposed huge financial costs on both superpowers, the Soviet Union was in a weaker economic position to cope with extremely high levels of military spending (see the US–Soviet economic comparison for 1989 on the next page). For most of the Cold War, the USSR's defence expenditure increased by between four and seven per cent each year. By the mid-1980s, the military budget accounted for about 25 per cent of Soviet GDP and 40 per cent of the state budget which represented a punishingly high financial commitment to defence in peacetime. Gorbachev realised that, without large cuts in defence spending to release funds for reform, economic and social conditions in the USSR could not be improved. Senior Red Army officers also recognised that the level of military spending was unsustainable. As the former Soviet military adviser Marshall Sergei Akhromeev recalled in 1996, 'The Soviet Union could no longer continue a policy of military confrontation with the United States and NATO after 1985. The economic possibilities for such a policy had been exhausted.'

| | |
|---|---|
| 1948 – 94.7 | 1970 – 346 |
| 1950 – 133 | 1975 – 242 |
| 1955 – 344.5 | 1980 – 246.2 |
| 1960 – 289.6 | 1985 – 343.7 |
| 1965 – 268.3 | 1990 – 358.7 |

US military spending 1948–90 (in billions of dollars at 1996 dollar values)

|  | USSR | USA |
|---|---|---|
| GDP ($) | 2 659 500 | 5 233 300 |
| Population | 291 million | 250 million |
| [etc] | | |

Comparison of the Soviet and US Economies (1989)

In the USA, military spending as a proportion of GDP averaged 10 per cent in the 1950s, nine per cent in the 1960s, five per cent in the 1970s (due to détente), and seven per cent in the 1980s. With its larger and more powerful economy, the US could afford to devote a smaller proportion of its resources to defence. Nevertheless, average annual US military spending during the Cold War amounted to $298.5 billion (at 1996 dollar values).

## The 'economic factors' interpretation: an overall assessment

| Strengths | This focuses on a key structural factor, which had an important bearing on the superpowers' ability to sustain their Cold War policies. |
|---|---|
| | This approach is particularly valuable in examining Soviet behaviour, bearing in mind how economic factors influenced Gorbachev's radically new approach to Cold War relations. |
| | It widens the debate about the end of the Cold War beyond the influence of particular leaders by focusing on long-term economic trends. |
| Weaknesses | Until Gorbachev came into power, Soviet leaders continued with Cold War policies even though economic problems were mounting. |
| | Reagan's 'overspend' strategy appeared to have little effect on Soviet behaviour between 1981 and 1985. |
| | Such an approach may underestimate the relative importance of Gorbachev and Reagan in bringing about superpower accommodation after 1985. |

## 'People power' in the Soviet Bloc

Without doubt, popular pressure or 'people power' in Eastern Europe played an important role in ending the Cold War. Growing disillusionment in the satellite states during the 1980s culminated in widespread protests and demonstrations, which broke the communist regimes' monopoly of power and dismantled the Soviet Bloc. It amounted to a very public rejection of Marxist-Leninism:

### Source 5
(From Joseph Smith, *The Cold War 1945–1991*, published by Blackwell 1998)

In 1989 the structure of international relations was dramatically transformed, not from 'above' but from 'below' by the 'revolutions' in Eastern Europe. The West looked on in amazement as the people of Eastern Europe spontaneously took the initiative in bringing about the peaceful overthrow of the Iron Curtain. A critical factor in their success was undoubtedly Gorbachev's decision not to resort to military force. His celebrated speech at the United Nations in December 1988 had stated that all nations possessed 'freedom of choice'. The people of Eastern Europe took him at his word and opted for the West as their preferred model of political, economic and moral progress.

The 'people power' interpretation is an explanation that focuses on the impact of events from 'below' rather than the influence of 'high politics' and the role of particular national leaders. It asserts that the mobilisation of popular discontent across Eastern Europe effectively ended the Cold War by removing the satellite regimes. This interpretation maintains that:

- The 1980s witnessed growing popular discontent in Eastern Europe due to the failure of central economic planning, continued repression and the moral bankruptcy of communism.

- Before 1989, popular opposition had secured concessions from the communist regimes, for example, the gains made by Solidarity and the Catholic Church in Poland 1980–1, and the start of the reform process in Hungary in 1988 (see below).

- 'People power' offers a central explanation for the transformation of Eastern Europe in 1989. Change occurred rapidly and peacefully (except in Romania), which points to a mass rejection of the satellite regimes and an almost complete loss of popular legitimacy.

One historian who sees the 'people power' argument as an important part of the explanation for the end of the Cold War is Joseph Smith.

### Why did popular discontent grow in Eastern Europe in the 1980s?
- Growing trade links with the West during the détente period of the 1970s encouraged many East Europeans to take an interest in capitalist methods and the free market. Those links also made citizens of the satellite states aware of higher Western living standards.

## Examiners' notes

Here you need to:

- understand the extent to which 'people power' in the Soviet Bloc was responsible for the end of the Cold War (make sure you are aware of the impact of popular pressure in several satellite states and try to identify common causes, features and consequences)

- identify the strengths and weaknesses of this perspective (for example, think about how 'people power' interacted with Gorbachev's policies, Soviet economic problems and the moral bankruptcy of communism).

## Examiners' notes

Source 5 is a good example of an extract that offers several potential areas of analysis regarding 'people power' in Eastern Europe at the end of the 1980s. If you read the source carefully, you can see that these popular demonstrations were spontaneous and took the West by surprise, effectively dismantled the Soviet Bloc, were encouraged by Gorbachev's refusal to intervene, and represented a widespread public demand for 'Western' reforms.

Make sure you extract all the relevant information from the sources you are given in the exam.

- East European living standards declined in the 1980s because of mounting economic problems. Prices and unemployment increased, housing, food and consumer goods were in short supply, the USSR cut back on subsidised oil and natural gas supplies to the satellite states, as world prices fell. In addition, large debts were owed to the West.

- Popular expectations raised by the USSR signing the Helsinki Accords (1975) were to be disappointed. The communist regimes of the Eastern Bloc continued to rely on political repression, censorship and other human rights abuses to keep themselves in power.

- There was resentment at continued religious persecution, and the galvanising impact of the appointment of Pope John Paul II mobilised Polish Catholics and boosted support for Solidarity.

- The growth of nationalism in Eastern Europe (particularly East Germany), which challenged the satellite states' 'official' loyalty to the international concept of communism and the USSR (as the birthplace of socialist revolution).

### Did 'people power' end the Cold War?

The contribution made by 'people power' to the end of the Cold War is yet another controversial area. Some of the main arguments on both sides of the debate are set out below.

**YES**

The nature of political change in Eastern Europe in 1989 also endorsed the 'people power' argument because:
- The speedy and largely peaceful removal of all the satellite regimes indicated an almost total collapse of popular legitimacy.
- Popular pressure pushed the process much further than Gorbachev wanted; the Soviet leader envisaged a liberalised socialist 'commonwealth' of East European states.

**YES**

Prior to 1989, growing discontent in Eastern Europe placed increasing pressure for change on the satellite states, and the USSR. For example, in 1980–1, when the Polish government registered the Catholic-backed independent trade union 'Solidarity', a wave of strikes and a revival of Solidarity occurred; the Hungarian government introduced multi-candidate elections in 1983 to try to compensate for economic problems. Five years later, Hungarian communists began talks on reform with other political parties, and in January 1989 Hungary became the first satellite state to set free elections for 1990.

**Did 'people power' end the Cold War?**

**YES**

Without Gorbachev's crucial intervention, events in Eastern Europe would have turned out very differently:
- He abandoned the Brezhnev Doctrine and advocated 'freedom of choice' (1988), which served as a clear signal to Eastern Europe.
- At crucial points in 1989, Gorbachev urged the Polish and East German communist regimes not to use force against protesters.

**NO**

The 'people power' argument is rather limited as an explanation for the end of the Cold War, as it underestimates:
- the overall impact of Gorbachev's radically new approach to Cold War diplomacy after 1985
- the consequences of Reagan's 'militarist counter-revolution' and subsequent accommodation with the USSR for Cold War relations.

### Examiners' notes

Here you need to:

- understand the extent to which the moral bankruptcy of Soviet communism was responsible for the end of the Cold War
- identify the strengths and weaknesses of this perspective and try to establish links between the moral bankruptcy viewpoint and other competing interpretations, for example, Reagan's hard-line policies.

### Examiners' notes

Here is another example of a single source offering more than one line of argument. If you were answering the question 'To what extent was the moral bankruptcy of the Soviet system responsible for the end of the Cold War in the 1980s?', and were given Source 6 to help you, you would need to be aware that this extract provides material to develop the moral bankruptcy viewpoint and the hard-line Reagan policy argument. The two could then be linked.

### Essential notes

During the Brezhnev era, alcohol consumption quadrupled. Prominent dissidents included: Soviet physicist Andrei Sakharov; Czech playwright, Vaclav Havel and founder of the Jewish movement, Anatoly Sharansky.

## The moral bankruptcy of communism

For many historians, the Soviet Bloc was also morally bankrupt. According to this view, a combination of factors including: a privileged and corrupt communist elite, an alienated population, abuse of human rights and reliance on military force had seriously eroded the legitimacy of communism by the early 1980s.

This undermining process helped to precipitate an internal collapse, which compelled the USSR and the satellite states to abandon the Cold War.

> **Source 6**
> (From John Lewis Gaddis, *'On Starting All Over Again: A Naïve Approach to the Study of the Cold War'* in Odd Arne Westad, *Reviewing the Cold War: Approaches, Interpretations, Theory*, Published by Frank Cass 2000)
>
> In 1983, Ronald Reagan denounced the Soviet Union as the 'focus of evil in the modern world'. It was a striking departure from an official rhetoric ... that had portrayed the USSR as operating within the same moral universe as the Western democracies ... Whatever one thought, one did not say. It is clear now, though, that citizens of the Soviet Union and its East European satellites saw the 'Evil Empire' speech rather differently. By the end of the decade, many of them had come to agree with Reagan that the regime under which they lived was, if not evil, then certainly illegitimate.

### A privileged and corrupt elite

A privileged and corrupt communist elite emerged in the USSR, particularly under Leonid Brezhnev's leadership from 1964 to 1982. Consequently, Soviet society was divided into two groups: the CPSU (Communist Party of the Soviet Union), which enjoyed preferential status, and the rest of society, which did not. Within the Communist Party, the *nomenklatura* in particular, enjoyed the trappings of office at national, regional and local levels. *Nomenklatura*, or Soviet elite, were the bureaucrats, appointed by the CPSU to administer all aspects of state activity. Depending on their rank, these bureaucrats had exclusive access to a range of privileges including country residences, official cars, private supplys of Western goods, luxury vacation resorts, and private medical centres. Many members of the *nomenklatura* took bribes, pocketed government funds and appointed family members and friends to state jobs. The satellite regimes of Eastern Europe were similarly led by privileged and frequently corrupt communist elites.

### An alienated population

In contrast, the ordinary citizens of the Soviet Bloc faced long working hours, low-grade housing, poorly stocked shops, shortages of basic foodstuffs and consumer goods, and a lack of amenities. These deficiencies led to:

- low productivity of the workforce
- an extensive black market
- growing social problems such as alcoholism, mental illness, and suicide.

In public, most people conformed to avoid the attention of the security police. Privately, most felt alienated from the communist regime that governed them and the authorities knew this. Secret research conducted by the USSR in the 1960s revealed that few Soviet citizens embraced Marxism–Leninism.

## Abuse of human rights

The Helsinki Accords (1975) committed the USSR to guarantee freedom of speech, protest and movement but Soviet leadership calculated that they could contain the 'human rights' issue within the Eastern Bloc. However, the Accords encouraged Russian and East European dissidents to condemn human rights abuses in the Soviet Bloc. Furthermore, groups such as the Helsinki watch committees and Charter 77 were established to monitor Soviet compliance. The Helsinki agreement on human rights gave the West a powerful ideological and moral weapon to use against communism.

Communist leaders largely ignored the Helsinki human rights provisions, fearing that greater freedom would undermine Marxist–Leninism and the Soviet Bloc.

Soviet and East European dissidents were imprisoned, harassed or exiled. Others were sent to labour camps. Some were declared insane, drugged and confined to mental institutions. Many Soviet Jews (known as refuseniks) were denied the right to emigrate to Israel or the USA.

## 'Empire by rape'

Ultimately, the Soviet Bloc was an 'empire by rape' – created and maintained by force rather than consent. From the outset, this undermined its legitimacy in the West and for many who were living under communist control. Red Army interventions in 1953, 1956 and 1968, to keep the Eastern Bloc in line, merely reinforced the point. In 1982, Reagan argued that the satellite regimes had had 30 years to establish their legitimacy and hold free elections, but had failed to do so because governments 'planted by bayonets do not take root'. The rapid collapse of the Eastern Bloc in 1988, in the absence of Red Army protection, confirms this.

## The 'moral bankruptcy' interpretation: an overall assessment

| | |
|---|---|
| **Strengths** | This focuses on a key structural factor, which undermined the USSR's ability to sustain its Cold War policies. |
| | This approach is particularly valuable in examining Soviet behaviour, bearing in mind how the legitimacy factor influenced Gorbachev's new approach to Cold War relations. It also informed Reagan's hard-line strategy in the early 1980s. |
| | It widens the debate beyond the influence of particular leaders by focusing on the long-term moral crisis within the Soviet Bloc. |
| **Weaknesses** | Until Gorbachev, Soviet leaders continued with Cold War policies even though the problem of moral bankruptcy became increasingly obvious. |
| | Reagan's moral stance on the USSR appeared to have little effect on Soviet behaviour between 1981 and 1985. |
| | This approach may underestimate the relative importance of Gorbachev and Reagan in bringing about superpower accommodation after 1985. |

---

**Essential notes**

Charter 77 was a group of 242 Czech intellectuals and ex-government officials, who issued a charter calling on the Czech authorities to observe the Helsinki Accords and the UN Declaration on Human Rights. The Czech government imprisoned many Charter 77 members.

**Essential notes**

Soviet Jews pressed for the freedom to leave the USSR and their campaign attracted worldwide publicity. As a result, the number of Jews allowed to emigrate increased from 14 000 (1975) to 51 000 (1979). However, Jewish emigration fell after the invasion of Afghanistan.

**Essential notes**

The 'moral bankruptcy' interpretation says that the illegitimacy of the Eastern Bloc undermined Soviet communism and caused its collapse in the late 1980s and that the Soviet Bloc's 'moral crisis' had several features: corrupt governing elites, populations disillusioned with Marxist–Leninist rule, disrespect for human rights and repressive political systems. This interpretation holds that this illegitimacy helps to explain the speed of political change across the Eastern Bloc in 1989.

Historians who have emphasised this view include John Lewis Gaddis and Michael Burleigh.

## Introduction

This section of the book covers the skills you must use to gain a high mark. Your Unit 3 exam will comprise of two parts: Section A and Section B. The Section A questions are essay questions, unlike the Section B questions, which are source-based. While you do need to have learned and understood the subject content, you won't get many marks for simply off-loading what you know. Each question will always have a specific focus and you need to be able to identify this, select the best evidence to use and then apply it in a suitable way. This guidance should help you do this better by:

- providing a general outline of the essay question
- recognising the different types of essay questions
- planning your answer
- writing effective introductions, main paragraphs and conclusions
- understanding the mark scheme.

## Answering a Section A question

### The essay question: a general outline

For Section A of the examination, you are required to select one of two essay questions and answer it. For Option E2 (Superpower Relations) the essay questions will be drawn from the Cold War areas:

- the post-Stalin thaw and the bid for peaceful co-existence: Khrushchev and the responses of Dulles, Eisenhower and Kennedy
- the arms race, 1949–63: nuclear technology, delivery systems, the Cuban missile crisis, the Test Ban Treaty
- Sino–Soviet relations, 1949–76: alliance to confrontation in Asia and its impact on US policy
- Détente, 1969–80: the Strategic Arms Limitations Talks (SALT) and agreements, Helsinki Accords, the impact of economic realities.

From the outset, it is very important to realise that an essay question can be set on one or more of these topics. For example, the essay question on the left, top, focuses on knowledge that is based only on the last bullet point in the text above.

However, the question on the left, bottom, requires knowledge that is based on the first *two* bullet points in the text above.

The essay question is marked against Assessment Objective 1a and 1b (AO1a and b), which means that you need to select relevant historical knowledge from what you have learned and use it to support an argument leading to a judgement on the question that has been set. In the exam, you should spend approximately 50 minutes (including about 5 minutes planning) answering the essay question. It is worth 30 marks.

### Example essay questions

*'US-Soviet Détente failed in the late 1970s primarily because of the Helsinki Accords.'*
*How far do you agree with this view?*

*To what extent was the post-Stalin thaw in superpower relations in the years 1953 to 1961 due to the nuclear arms race?*

## Recognising the different types of essay questions

Section A essay questions are divided into:

- causal questions – requiring you to write an analysis of the causes or causes and consequences of an historical event or development

- judgement questions – requiring you to make and justify an historical judgement about the significance of a particular event, individual or development.

## Causal questions

There are three main types of causal questions that can appear in Section A.

### 1. Single-focus

A single-focus causal question requires an explanation for one event, issue or episode. The causal analysis is demanding in the question on the right, top, because of the need to analyse and explain 'so rapidly'.

### 2. Double-focus

The double-focus causal question requires you to consider two specific sets of causes or reasons. In the example on the right, centre, you must focus on 'ideological divisions' and 'conflicting national interests'. You must cover both parts of the question adequately or your answer will be unbalanced.

### 3. Indirect

An indirect causal question does not have an obvious causal question stem. It makes a claim about causes, which you assess by examining the causes stated in the question and other causes drawn from your own knowledge. In the question on the right, bottom, for instance, any consideration of 'the Americans' good fortune' should lead to a discussion of the serious deterioration of Sino–Soviet relations in the 1960s *and* Mao's decision to seek better relations with the USA.

### Causal questions: dos and don'ts

| Do | Don't |
|---|---|
| ✓ Establish clearly the relative importance of the causal factors considered – *this is very important.* | ✗ Attempt to use a narrative structure to answer a causal question. |
| ✓ Show, where relevant, how causal factors interacted. | |
| ✓ Structure your essay around the causal factors selected for discussion. | |

## 1. Single-focus

*Why did the US–Soviet nuclear arms race develop so rapidly in the years 1949 to 1961?*

## 2. Double–focus

*'Ideological divisions were more important than conflicting national interests in explaining why Sino–Soviet relations deteriorated in the years 1958 to 1969.'*
*How far do you agree with this view?*

## 3. Indirect

*'The US rapprochement with China in the early 1970s owed more to the Americans' good fortune than to their Cold War diplomacy.'*
*How far do you agree with this view?*

## 1. One-Part

*'US–Soviet tensions were considerably heightened in the 1970s.'*
*How far do you agree with this view?*

## 2. Two-Part

*'Destabilising yet vital for superpower security'*
*How far do you agree with this judgement on the impact of the nuclear arms race on Cold War relations in the years 1949 to 1962?*

## 3. Causes/consequences

*To what extent were the changes in US–Soviet relations in the years 1953 to 1960 determined by President Eisenhower's 'New Look' policy?*

## 4. Change

*To what extent did US–Soviet relations improve in the years 1953 to 1960?*

## 5. Mixed

*Why, and how profoundly, did divisions appear in Sino–Soviet relations between 1958 and 1969?*

## Judgement questions

Judgement questions typically start: 'To what extent …?', 'How far do you agree that …?', 'How important …?' or 'Examine the validity of the claim that …'.

There are five main types of judgement questions that may appear in Section A.

### 1. One-part

You are required to put forward and support a *single* judgement. In this case, you need to make a judgement about the extent to which US–Soviet tensions were heightened in the 1970s.

### 2. Two-part

You are required to offer and support *two separate* judgements. In the example on the left, you need to consider and reach a judgement on the 'destabilising' and 'security' aspects of the nuclear arms race. A constructive approach to this type of question is to split the main analysis into two separate sections, to offer and support a judgement on each aspect.

### 3. Causes/consequences

Some judgement questions, as in the example on the left, may ask you to make a judgement about causes and/or consequences.

### 4. Change

Other judgement questions may ask you to make a judgement about the extent or nature of change over a given period. In the example on the left, you are asked to make a judgement about the extent to which US–Soviet relations improved in the seven years following Stalin's death. With this type of question it is important to establish clear criteria that you will use to measure the extent or nature of change.

### 5. Mixed

Occasionally, mixed causal and judgement questions can appear in Section A, as per the example on the left. With this type of question, you could divide your answer into two sections. One part should analyse the causes and the other should offer and support a judgement.

### Judgement questions: dos and don'ts

| Do | Don't |
|---|---|
| ✓ Make an explicit judgement that clearly answers the question set (e.g. US–Soviet tensions were not heightened/were heightened to some degree/were considerably heightened in the 1970s) – *this is very important*. | ✗ Attempt to use a narrative structure to answer a judgement question. |
| ✓ Structure your essay around the analytical points selected for discussion. | ✗ Forget to offer an overall judgement. |
| ✓ Show, where relevant, the links between the analytical points that have been developed in the process of forming a judgement. | ✗ Offer an implicit or brief judgement. |

## Planning your answer

### Causal questions

When planning an answer to a causal question, it's very important that you follow these steps.

- Structure your answer on the causal factors selected.

- Show how causal factors interacted.

- Establish the relative importance of the causal factors considered.

The diagram below shows some of the relevant causal factors that you could select to answer the causal question on the right:

### Example causal question

*Why did the US–Soviet nuclear arms race develop so rapidly in the years 1949–61?*

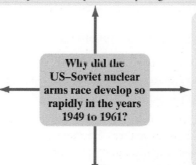

The nuclear arms race generated its own **'vicious circle' momentum** as each superpower developed increasingly advanced weapons to match or pull ahead of its rival and so **guarantee its security**. For example, Soviet acquisition of nuclear weapons (1949) led the US to develop the more powerful hydrogen bomb (1952).

**National and personal prestige** also played a role. The nuclear arms race became part of the wider ideological competition to demonstrate the superiority of US capitalism or Soviet communism (which implied continual technological development). Some Cold War leaders, such as Khrushchev, also attempted to use their side's 'lead' in the nuclear arms race as propaganda to enhance their personal prestige.

**Why did the US–Soviet nuclear arms race develop so rapidly in the years 1949 to 1961?**

The **culture of secrecy and suspicion** surrounding the development of these weapons led both superpowers to exaggerate the other's nuclear capability and fear they were lagging behind (e.g. US concerns over a 'missile gap' in the late 1950s). This mentality accelerated the arms race.

The **military-industrial complex** in both countries had obvious economic and political motives for accelerating the nuclear arms race by emphasising the threat posed by the other side. Eisenhower, for example, warned the USA in the early 1960s of the 'unwarranted influence' of the military-industrial complex. In 1960, annual US military spending stood at $50 billion (10 per cent of GDP and 52 per cent of the federal budget).

An effective plan here would be as follows.

- Structure the main section into four paragraphs, each of which would analyse the role played by one of the selected causal factors in developing the nuclear arms race so rapidly.

- Show where the factors interact, for example, the 'match or pull ahead' momentum of the US–Soviet nuclear arms race was partly fuelled by the culture of secrecy and suspicion because neither superpower could be exactly sure where it stood in relation to the other's nuclear capability.

- Establish the relative importance of the causal factors considered, for example, you could argue that the US and Soviet need for security was the most important factor because the other three causal factors all relate in some way to superpower defence against threats.

*Judgement questions*

When planning an answer to a judgement question, it's very important that you follow these steps:

- Make an explicit judgement that clearly answers the question set.

- Structure your essay around the analytical points selected for discussion.

- Show, where relevant, the links between the analytical points that have been developed in the process of forming a judgement.

### Example judgement question

*'US–Soviet tensions were considerably heightened in the 1970s.'*
*How far do you agree with this view?*

The spectrum below shows a partially completed 'judgement continuum' that would help you to answer the judgement question on the left:

| Not heightened/improved | Heightened to some degree | Considerably heightened |
| --- | --- | --- |
| SALT I (1972) Improved US–Soviet trade (1974–5) | 1975 Helsinki Accords (Basket 3 – human rights) | Soviet invasion of Afghanistan (1979) |

This 'judgement continuum' is an excellent planning tool because it:

- focuses on the critical element – making a judgement

- allows you to put the historical evidence into relevant judgement categories that provide an ideal structure for the main section of your essay.

Once completed, the spectrum will help you to reach an overall judgement.

With this particular question, after you have placed all the relevant evidence from the 1970s in the appropriate judgement category (not heightened/considerably heightened), you can then make an overall judgement on 'considerably heightened'. This could be based, for example, on the category containing the largest amount of evidence. Alternatively, it might be based on the date of the evidence in each category (for example, early 1970s evidence indicates 'not heightened/improved' but later 1970s evidence reveals 'considerably heightened tension').

### Writing effective introductions, main paragraphs and conclusions

#### The introduction

A good introduction is very important when you are answering an essay question, partly because it is the first impression you make with the examiner. Treat it as a golden opportunity to impress with your understanding of what the question is asking you to do and how you aim to answer it. Spend about 5–7 minutes – but no longer – writing this opening paragraph. A good introduction should aim to fulfil these functions.

- Set out clearly your understanding of what the question is asking you to do.

- Identify the range of factors you intend to discuss in the main section.

- Offer a provisional judgement, so the examiner knows the line of argument you intend to take.

- Define any key words in the question and explain the significance of any dates that have been included.

The passage below is a strong introduction to the question on the right:

**Example question**

*To what extent was the deterioration in Sino–Soviet relations in the years 1958 to 1969 due to ideological divisions?*

> After the establishment of the PRC in 1949, many in the West assumed that the USSR and China would form a monolithic Eurasian communist bloc. Initially, this seemed to be borne out by the 1950 Treaty of Friendship and Sino–Soviet support for communist North Korea's attack on South Korea (1950). By 1958, however, Sino–Soviet relations had become strained and, over the next decade, deteriorated almost to the point of war. This growing rift between the PRC and the USSR was due to three interrelated factors, which will be examined in this essay. First, ideological differences over the 'correct path' to communism led both powers to accuse the other of abandoning Marxist–Leninism. Second, personality clashes between Mao and the two Soviet leaders during this period – Khrushchev and Brezhnev – added another corrosive element. Finally, competing national interests, partly due to the fact that the PRC and the USSR shared a common border, also served to damage relations. Ultimately, rival national interests were more important than either ideological differences or personality clashes in undermining Sino–Soviet relations. Although divisions were often expressed in ideological and personal terms, Sino–Soviet differences really stemmed from the fact that both states were determined to pursue self-interested national policies.

This is an effective introduction for three reasons.

1. The opening sentences briefly but clearly set out the basic Sino–Soviet relationship during the 1950s and 1960s. This is not strictly necessary but it immediately indicates that the student has a clear grasp of the issue to be explained.

2. The middle section clearly identifies ideological divisions and two other relevant factors that will be analysed to reach a judgement on the deteriorating Sino–Soviet relationship.

3. The final sentences offer a provisional judgement about the extent to which ideological divisions damaged Sino–Soviet relations.

### *The main section*

The main section is a crucial part of your essay because this is where you develop the detailed analysis essential for answering the question. Try to write four to six substantial paragraphs in this part of your response. Each paragraph in the main section should:

- support the opening point with examples from your own knowledge and then make clear how this adds weight to your argument (Point–Evidence–Explanation–Evaluation)

- address a new point
- link back to previous points, where possible, to show that you understand the connections
- follow on naturally from the one before.

Finish each point by linking back to the wording of the question in some way. This should guarantee that you are addressing the question directly.

Following the Sino–Soviet question on the previous page (see section on *Introduction*), this is a good main section paragraph.

> A key area of ideological division emerged in the late 1950s over the Soviet policy of peaceful co-existence. This policy was based on the premise that any direct conflict with the West was likely to result in nuclear annihilation; therefore the Soviets sought to reach a diplomatic accommodation with the Americans, assuming that the Marxist dialectic would hold true and that capitalism would inevitably collapse. Therefore, rather than continually confronting the US, the Soviets engaged in a series of meetings and summits in the late 1950s (Camp David) and 1960s (Vienna). Mao regarded this rapprochement with the West as a betrayal of the revolutionary struggle. He believed in the notion of permanent revolution – that there should be an ongoing (and even nuclear) struggle with the capitalist powers, in an attempt to spread communism across the developing world. This confrontational approach was most dramatically seen in the Taiwan Straits crisis of 1958 when Mao was reluctant to back down from bombing the nationalist-held islands, despite being threatened with a nuclear response by US Secretary of State Dulles. The key issue here is that ideology caused a breach in Sino–Soviet relations because it led both sides to adopt conflicting policies in their relations with the US, which neither could tolerate. Whilst Khrushchev regarded Mao's approach as an unacceptably reckless strategy, Mao viewed the Soviets with increasing contempt as they appeared to be abandoning the revolutionary struggle.

This is an effective main section paragraph for the following reasons:

- It begins by introducing the central point – the ideological divisions brought about by the policy of peaceful co-existence (see red text).
- Clear explanations of why the USSR adopted this policy and why Mao rejected it are offered (see blue text).
- Relevant evidence (see green text) is included to support these explanations.
- Finally, an evaluation is made as to the importance of peaceful co-existence in fostering Sino–Soviet ideological divisions (see purple text).

### The conclusion
For A2 level, the conclusion has to be more than a summary of what you have said. Rather, it needs to be the culmination of your understanding of issues established in the introduction, the arguments examined and assessed, and the evaluative judgement resulting from this. Don't skimp on this section – spend a good 5 minutes on it. For many students it may be the key part of the essay in determining the level awarded, as it is where you actually answer the question and weigh up your analysis.

A good conclusion will:

- round off all the points you have already made in your argument and make it clear why you have argued your case in this particular way

- reach a clear judgement, for example, the relative importance of factors

- consider the themes running through your essay and how they link – demonstrating your understanding that historical issues and factors do not act in isolation to each other

- avoid throwing in a brand new point at this stage – it's too late!

Still on the Sino–Soviet question, this is a strong conclusion.

Ideological divisions certainly contributed to the deterioration in Sino–Soviet relations between 1958 and 1969. Both the USSR and the PRC considered themselves to be the 'authentic' communist state and each regarded its rival as 'un-Marxist'. This led, for instance, to strident criticism of the Soviet policy of peaceful co-existence and Mao's peasant-based political philosophy. Even the personality clashes had distinctly ideological overtones, particularly in the period up to 1964, when Khrushchev and Mao openly vied for leadership of the world communist movement. Nevertheless, ideological divisions played a subordinate role to competing national interests in undermining Sino–Soviet relations. Both powers used the language of ideological differences to mask the pursuit of national interests, expanded spheres of influence and state security. Thus Mao's 'ideological' criticism of peaceful co-existence and the early stages of détente (after the Cuban missile crisis) reflected the PRC's concern that a US Soviet accommodation would jeopardise its security and leave it isolated. Similarly, Mao's encouragement of greater Albanian and Romanian independence was condemned by Khrushchev as an attempt to divide the world communist movement when in fact the USSR was more concerned about the threat this posed to its own sphere of influence. Ultimately, although ideological divisions were important, competing national interests played a greater role in eroding Sino–Soviet relations.

This is an effective conclusion because it begins its overall judgement by assessing the extent to which ideological divisions played a role in the deteriorating Sino–Soviet relationship. A sophisticated feature here is the relevant link made between ideological and personal rivalry, which shows awareness of the interrelationship between the factors under discussion.

It then moves on to make its key judgement about the importance of competing national interest. Once again, this is linked relevantly to ideological divisions, but this time, to show how the latter were used as a smokescreen for policies of national self-interest.

The final sentence clearly reiterates the key judgement.

### Understanding the mark scheme

The examiner puts each essay into one of five levels, according to the criteria in the table overleaf. Your answer is then moved within the level (low, mid or high), depending on how well it meets the descriptor.

Obviously, you want your answer to go into the highest possible level, therefore it is worth becoming familiar with the table, so that you know what the examiners are looking for.

| Level | Level descriptor | Descriptor comments | Comments/example |
|---|---|---|---|
| **Level 1**<br><br>Simple statements<br><br>1–6 marks | Students will produce a series of statements, some of which may be simplified. The statements will be supported by factual material, which has some accuracy and relevance although not directed at the focus of the question. The material will be mostly generalised.<br><br>Low: 1–2 marks, mid: 3–4 marks, high: 5–6 marks | A level 1 answer is typically based on a limited amount of material and deals with the topic rather than the focus of the question.<br><br>Knowledge is generalised with few examples to support the statements. | A typical level 1 response to the question: *'Détente heightened US–Soviet tensions in the 1970s.' How far do you agree with this view?* would contain material about détente but would not address the 'heightened US–Soviet tensions' focus. |
| **Level 2**<br><br>Statements with some development<br><br>7–12 marks | Students will produce statements with some development in the form of mostly accurate and relevant factual material. There will be some analysis, but focus on the analytical demand of the question will be largely implicit. Candidates will attempt to make links between the statements and the material but is unlikely to be developed very far.<br><br>Low: 7–8 marks, mid: 9–10 marks, high: 11–12 marks | Level 2 answers can provide reasonably extensive information but often in the form of a narrative or a description.<br><br>There is some attempt to link the material to the question but it will not be explicit, links are assumed/answer is narrative.<br><br>The range of evidence is limited and links are asserted, rather than supported with information. | A level 2 response to the question given above, for example, will contain statements on détente which will have either (a) only implicit reference to heightened US–Soviet tension or (b) an argument based on insufficient evidence. Links to the question focus will be asserted, rather than shown. The student may maintain that the Helsinki Accords heightened tension without offering developed comments – for example, assuming it to be self-evident that continued Soviet human rights abuses heightened tension. |
| **Level 3**<br><br>Attempts analysis<br><br>13–18 marks | Students' answers will be broadly analytical and will show some understanding of the focus of the question. They may, however, include material, which is either descriptive, and thus only implicitly relevant to the question's focus, or which strays from that focus in places. Factual material will be accurate, but it may not consistently display depth and/or relevance.<br><br>Low: 13–14 marks, mid: 15–16 marks, high: 17–18 marks | In a level 3 response, the majority of the paragraphs will have a relevant point, some supporting evidence and related comment linked to the question. There will, however, be some weaker passages that may drift into narrative, lack a clear link to the question, include irrelevant material or lack analytical depth. | A typical level 3 response to the question: *Why did the US–Soviet nuclear arms race develop so rapidly in the years 1949–63?* will contain paragraphs with relevant causal analysis (on, perhaps, the impact of the Soviet nuclear test of 1949, the culture of secrecy surrounding nuclear weapons programmes and the development of rocket technology). It will also have weaker passages (such as a narrative section on, say, the development of the hydrogen bomb or an irrelevant section on peaceful co-existence). |

| Level | Level descriptor | Descriptor comments | Comments/example |
|---|---|---|---|
| **Level 4**<br>Analytical response<br>19–24 marks | Students offer an analytical response, which relates well to the focus of the question and which shows some understanding of the key issues contained in it with some evaluation of argument. The analysis will be supported by accurate factual material, which will be mostly relevant to the question asked. The selection of material may lack balance in places.<br><br>Low: 19–20 marks, mid: 21–22 marks, high: 23–24 marks | At level 4, a student's response will offer an analysis of the issues raised by the question.<br><br>The answer draws out the key points with detailed knowledge used to develop an argument.<br><br>There may be a little drifting from the specific question or a lack of balance with some aspects dealt with only briefly, the response may be a bit inconsistent.<br><br>The answer will show some attempt to evaluate the evidence used in the argument. | A level 4 answer to the question: *To what extent were the changes in US–Soviet relations in the years 1953–60 determined by President Eisenhower's 'New Look' policy?* will deal with the stated factor (the 'New Look' policy) and explore the ways Eisenhower's approach had an impact on US–Soviet relations. The student will also appreciate that the question requires other factors to be considered, such as the Soviet pursuit of peaceful co-existence and the nuclear arms race. The answer will not lose sight of the question focus but it may lack balance. |
| **Level 5**<br>Sustained analysis<br>25–30 marks | Students offer a sustained analysis, which directly addresses the focus of the question. They demonstrate explicit understanding of the key issues raised by the question, evaluating arguments and – as appropriate – interpretations. The analysis will be supported by an appropriate range and depth of accurate and well-selected factual material.<br><br>Low: 25–26 marks, mid: 27–28 marks, high: 29–30 marks | At level 5, the student's analysis is developed, balanced and sustained.<br><br>The answer draws out the key points and develops an argument with detailed knowledge.<br><br>The answer is well structured and discusses the evidence used to support, reject or modify the statement in the question.<br><br>The answer evaluates the interpretations and arguments. | In the question above, dealing with US–Soviet relations from 1953 to 1960, a level 5 answer will fully explore a range of factors. For example, in examining the view that US–Soviet relations during this period were determined by the Soviet pursuit of peaceful co-existence or the nuclear arms race, the student will show that both of these can be related to Eisenhower's 'New Look' policy. Thus, the implications of US policy will be explored beyond the more obvious features such as 'rollback', 'brinkmanship' and 'massive retaliation'. The response will offer an evaluative analysis with a balanced debate on the proposition contained in the question. |

## Answering a Section B question

The Section B question has a different focus than the Section A question. In the Section A question you are required to use your own knowledge (AO1) to complete the answer. In contrast, the Section B question requires you to reach a judgement about a claim by integrating your own knowledge (AO1) with interpretations offered by the sources (AO2b).

The Section B question focuses on the two controversies that you have studied. You must select from two questions, each of which refers to one of these controversies. Each question will be accompanied by three secondary sources. The sources will offer different interpretations relating to the controversies that you have studied.

### Choosing the question

Begin by reading both questions. If you immediately have a clear preference, skim-read the three sources that accompany that question (looking for key words, names and dates, and ensuring that you understand the interpretations offered) before you commit yourself.

Significantly, questions often contain a quote from one of the sources or paraphrase an interpretation put forward by a source. Therefore, it is a good idea to start by identifying the source referred to in the question. Skim-reading and looking for the source referred to in the question should enable you to check that you have understood the question correctly, and will help you as you plan your answer.

If you have no clear preference, then read the sources for each question carefully and base your choice on which set of sources you can understand most clearly. You should have left yourself 1 hour and 10 minutes to complete this question, so you can spend 5 minutes making sure that you have made the right choice.

### Planning your answer

Once you have selected the question it is very important to spend some time planning your answer. To access level 3 or above, you need to link your own knowledge to the sources. It is almost impossible to do this successfully without planning. Make sure that you leave enough time to do this and remember to think carefully about the main issues raised by the question. You can find an example of a plan on page 109.

### How do you work out the interpretation of the sources?

All of the sources in this unit will be secondary sources. Your task is to understand the interpretations that they offer. Therefore, it is useful to highlight and annotate the sources as you read them.

Some sources will contain more than one interpretation. For example, they may contain an argument and a counterargument. Other sources may only offer one interpretation. In either case, it is crucial to understand the interpretation the source offers.

In order to help you to understand how to identify an interpretation, look at the secondary sources that accompany the example question in the margin on the opposite page.

Having read the question, read each source and underline or highlight the key interpretations that the sources offer. It is important to work out which sources support and challenge the interpretation offered in the question. You could use different colours to indicate this:

- Use one colour to indicate the parts of the source that *support the interpretation* offered in the question.

- Use a second colour to indicate the parts of the source that *contradict the interpretation* offered in the question.

- Use a third colour to indicate the parts of the source that offer an *alternative interpretation*.

**Example question**

*How far do you agree that the Cold War came to end in the 1980s due to the USA's economic superiority?*

---

**Source 1**

(From Eric Hobsbawm, *Age of Extremes: The Short Twentieth Century 1914–1991*, published by Michael Joseph 1994)

Both superpowers overstretched and distorted their economies by a massive and enormously expensive competitive arms race, but the capitalist system could absorb the 3 trillion dollars of debt – essentially for military spending – into which the 1980s plunged the USA. There was nobody to take the equivalent strain on Soviet expenditure, which, in any case, represented a far higher proportion of Soviet production (perhaps 25 per cent) than the 7 per cent of the enormous US GDP* which went on the military in the mid-1980s. Furthermore, the Soviets' allies and dependants never walked on their own feet. They remained a constant and vast annual drain of tens of billions of dollars on the USSR. As for technology, as Western superiority grew dramatically, there was no contest.

---

Agreement with the interpretation offered by the question (yellow):

- 'but the capitalist system [i.e. the USA] could absorb the 3 trillion dollars of debt'

- 'There was nobody to take the equivalent strain on Soviet expenditure'

- 'the Soviets' allies and dependants never walked on their own feet'.

Contradiction to the interpretation offered by the source (green):

- 'Both superpowers overstretched and distorted their economies'.

Alternative interpretation offered by the source (turquoise):

- 'As for technology, as Western superiority grew dramatically, there was no contest'.

The question suggests that US economic superiority was the main factor that brought about the end of the Cold War. Hobsbawm's text largely supports this. However, there is evidence in the source that, despite its economic superiority, the Cold War was putting economic strain on the USA and, therefore, it was in the USA's interests to end the Cold War. The source also makes reference to the superior nature of Western technology.

## Example question

*How far do you agree that the Cold War came to end in the 1980s due to the USA's economic superiority?*

Now repeat the exercise with the same question, using the following source:

### Source 2

(From John Lewis Gaddis, *The Cold War*, published by Penguin 2005)

For Gorbachev, any attempt to maintain control over unwilling peoples through the use of force would degrade the Soviet system by overstretching its resources, discrediting its ideology, and resisting the irresistible forces of democratisation that were sweeping the world. He announced to the United Nations General Assembly, on 7 December 1988, that the Soviet Union would unilaterally cut its ground force commitment to the Warsaw Pact by half a million men. It suddenly became apparent, just as Reagan was leaving office, that the Reagan Doctrine had been pushing against an open door. But Gorbachev had also made it clear, to the peoples and the governments of Eastern Europe, that the door was now open.

Agreement with the interpretation offered by the question (yellow):

- 'any attempt to maintain control over unwilling peoples … would degrade the Soviet system by overstretching its resources'.

Alternative interpretation offered by the source (turquoise):

- discrediting its ideology
- 'the Reagan Doctrine'
- 'Gorbachev had also made it clear … that the door [that is, freedom from Soviet control] was now open'.

### Integrating sources and cross-referencing

It is really important that you do not simply work through the sources one by one, because this kind of answer is unlikely to achieve more than level 2 in either assessment objective. You should try to treat the sources as a set and use them together. You will find that there are points of disagreement between the interpretations offered by the sources, as well as points of agreement. Where possible, you should cross-reference these points.

To help you to understand how to go about the task of integration, you will be examining Source 3, together with those above.

### Source 3

(From Michael Burleigh, *Sacred Causes: Religion and Politics from the European Dictators to Al Qaeda*, published by HarperPress 2006)

Reagan restored a moral tone to international affairs, most memorably when in March 1983 he referred to the USSR as the 'evil empire'. While that led the Soviets to imagine that they were dealing with a US president crazed enough to launch the bomb, in fact Reagan had a horror of nuclear weapons, and consistently urged on the Soviets the need to remove them through effective anti-ballistic missile defences. That offer in the form of the Strategic Defence Initiative (for deterrence had relied on the absence of just these systems) unlocked the Cold War by denying its permanence and forcing the Russians to realise that they could never compete with America in the most advanced computer and laser technologies.

Begin by looking for areas of agreement and disagreement between the three sources provided for the question on page 105.

Ways in which the sources agree:

- Source 1 and Source 2 focus on Soviet economic problems. Source 1 notes that the USSR could not compete with the USA in terms of defence spending, while Source 2 argues that Gorbachev was reluctant to assert control over Eastern Europe for fear of over-stretching the resources of the USSR.

- Source 1 and Source 3 agree on the technological battle fought between the USA and the USSR. Both sources agree on the superiority of Western technology, and Source 3 explicitly links this to the Strategic Defence Initiative (SDI).

- Source 2 and Source 3 agree on the importance of personalities in ending the Cold War. Source 2 highlights Gorbachev's willingness to relax control over Eastern Europe, while Source 3 focuses on Reagan's approach to international affairs.

Ways in which the sources disagree:

- Source 2 and Source 3 place different levels of importance on the two leaders. Source 3 indicates that Reagan's foreign policy and his pursuit of SDI were important in ending the Cold War, whereas Source 2 argues that Reagan was 'pushing against an open door', noting that Gorbachev was responsible for the fundamental change that led to the end of the Cold War.

- Source 1 and Source 2 are different in that Source 1 stresses the significance of the economic imbalance between the USA and the USSR, whereas Source 2 mentions a series of factors, including economics, ideology, Reagan and Gorbachev.

## The role of your own knowledge

Although the sources will drive your argument, you need to include relevant, specific and detailed own knowledge to support your argument. You can use your own knowledge in three main ways:

1. You can expand on a point that has already been made in the sources. For example, you could pick up on Source 3's point that Reagan 'restored a moral tone to international affairs' by noting that he believed that détente was 'a communist trick' and that he used foreign policy to weaken the USSR by restricting trade and therefore denying them access to high-tech Western goods.

2. You can challenge a point that has been made in the sources. For example, Source 3 argues that one of the reasons why the Russians ended the Cold War was their realisation 'that they could never compete with America in the most advanced computer and laser technologies'. However, you could point out that Gorbachev was keen to end SDI through diplomacy without necessarily ending the Cold War. In this sense, Russian policymakers were trying to end SDI rather than trying to end the Cold War.

3. Finally, you can use your own knowledge to put forward an interpretation that is not mentioned in the sources, but which draws on information provided by the sources. For example, Source 2 mentions ideology without developing it as an explanation for why the Cold War ended. You could use your own knowledge to argue that ideology played a crucial role, as the 'New Thinking' embraced by Gorbachev recognised that important elements of the communist system were no longer working and needed to be reformed. Furthermore, you could link this to Source 2's argument that Gorbachev played a crucial role in ending the Cold War.

The following paragraph is an example of how to integrate sources and own knowledge. Source material appears in black, own knowledge appears in blue. Note how well the student uses knowledge to develop the point that the USA could cope better with the economic strains of the Cold War.

Source 1 clearly argues that the US's economic superiority was a major reason why the Cold War ended. In essence, it argues that the US's economy could cope much better with the economic strains of the Cold War. By contrast, as Source 2 acknowledges, the Soviet economy was continually 'overstretching its resources.' The disparity between the two economies was decades old. However, in the late 1970s the USSR's rate of economic growth declined dramatically, from 5.7% in 1973 to around 1% in 1979. At the same time, the US's economy was recovering from the OPEC crisis, thanks to institutions such as the G7, which helped to stabilise international markets. As a result, by 1980 the contrast between the economies of the two superpowers was stark. Indeed, Soviet GDP was only 37% of the GDP of the USA. Moreover, Source 1 indicates a second area of economic superiority: capitalism was far better at innovation than communism, and that is why 'there was no contest' between the US and Soviet Technology. Specifically, as Source 2 shows, the USA had 'the most advanced computer and laser technologies' and these were exactly the sort of technologies that were necessary in the final phase of the arms race. Achieving nuclear parity with the US had cost the USSR an enormous '25 per cent' (Source 1) of its total spending. But competing with SDI would be impossible, as the USSR's economy could produce neither the wealth nor the high-tech goods necessary to match the US. In this sense, Source 1 is correct in that US economic superiority is one reason for the ending of the Cold War because the economy takes the 'strain on Soviet expenditure' caused by competition with the US.

When you are using your own knowledge to develop a point in the sources, make sure you link the point clearly to your discussion of the sources. The easiest way to do this is to add your own knowledge to your plan once you have finished studying the sources. You could plan in two colours, using one for the sources and another for own knowledge.

### Producing a plan

Your plan should focus on the interpretations put forward in the sources. It should also integrate sources and own knowledge. A plan for the question discussed above could look like the example on the opposite page. References to the sources are shown in black, own knowledge is shown in blue.

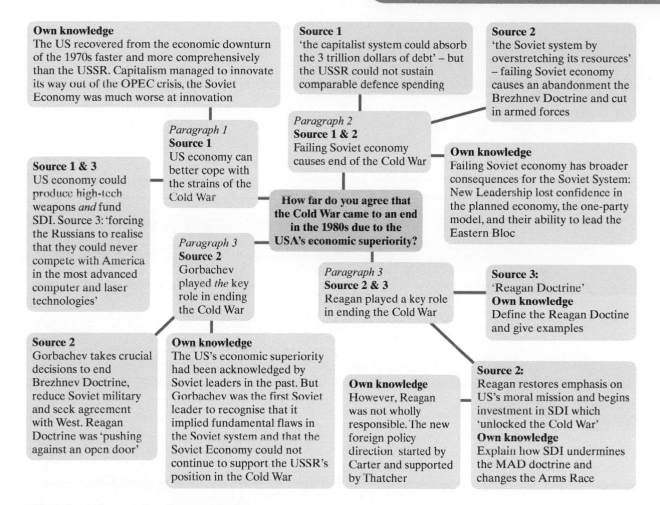

**Own knowledge**
The US recovered from the economic downturn of the 1970s faster and more comprehensively than the USSR. Capitalism managed to innovate its way out of the OPEC crisis, the Soviet Economy was much worse at innovation

**Source 1**
'the capitalist system could absorb the 3 trillion dollars of debt' – but the USSR could not sustain comparable defence spending

**Source 2**
'the Soviet system by overstretching its resources' – failing Soviet economy causes an abandonment the Brezhnev Doctrine and cut in armed forces

*Paragraph 1*
**Source 1**
US economy can better cope with the strains of the Cold War

*Paragraph 2*
**Source 1 & 2**
Failing Soviet economy causes end of the Cold War

**Own knowledge**
Failing Soviet economy has broader consequences for the Soviet System: New Leadership lost confidence in the planned economy, the one-party model, and their ability to lead the Eastern Bloc

**Source 1 & 3**
US economy could produce high-tech weapons *and* fund SDI. Source 3: 'forcing the Russians to realise that they could never compete with America in the most advanced computer and laser technologies'

**How far do you agree that the Cold War came to an end in the 1980s due to the USA's economic superiority?**

*Paragraph 3*
**Source 2**
Gorbachev played *the* key role in ending the Cold War

*Paragraph 3*
**Source 2 & 3**
Reagan played a key role in ending the Cold War

**Source 3:**
'Reagan Doctrine'
**Own knowledge**
Define the Reagan Doctine and give examples

**Source 2**
Gorbachev takes crucial decisions to end Brezhnev Doctrine, reduce Soviet military and seek agreement with West. Reagan Doctrine was 'pushing against an open door'

**Own knowledge**
The US's economic superiority had been acknowledged by Soviet leaders in the past. But Gorbachev was the first Soviet leader to recognise that it implied fundamental flaws in the Soviet system and that the Soviet Economy could not continue to support the USSR's position in the Cold War

**Own knowledge**
However, Reagan was not wholly responsible. The new foreign policy direction started by Carter and supported by Thatcher

**Source 2:**
Reagan restores emphasis on US's moral mission and begins investment in SDI which 'unlocked the Cold War'
**Own knowledge**
Explain how SDI undermines the MAD doctrine and changes the Arms Race

## What does the mark scheme mean?

The mark scheme means that you are required to show a number of skills. You need to be aware of the requirements of the question and how the mark scheme works in order to maximise your chances of doing well.

## The Assessment Objectives

Section B counts for 40 of the 70 marks. It examines two Assessment Objectives.

- First, your essay is marked against Assessment Objective 1a and 1b (AO1a and b), for a possible 16 marks. It assesses your ability to select relevant historical knowledge from what you have learned and your ability to use it to support an argument leading to a judgement about the question that has been set. This is the same skill as in Section A. However, Section B includes sources, so you will have to integrate source material with your own knowledge. Examples of this have been provided overleaf.

- Second, your essay is marked against Assessment Objective 2b (AO2b), for a possible 24 marks. It assesses your ability to analyse and evaluate judgements about the past. In this context, this means analysing and evaluating the interpretations provided by the sources. It does not require you to consider the reliability of the sources.

## The mark scheme for AO2b

| Level | Level descriptor | Descriptor comments | Example |
|---|---|---|---|
| **Level 1**<br><br>1–4 marks | Comprehends the surface features of sources and selects from them in order to identify points, which support or differ from the view posed in the question. When reaching a decision in relation to the question the sources will be used singly and in the form of a summary of their information. Own knowledge of the issue under debate will be presented as information but not integrated with the provided material.<br><br>Low: 1–2 marks, high: 3–4 marks | A level 1 answer will generally contain a few brief quotations lifted from the sources, which have not always been understood. It is very likely that the student will have worked through the sources in sequence. | A typical level 1 response answering the question: '*How far do you agree that the Cold War came to end in the 1980s due to the USA's economic superiority?*' would copy passages from the sources, or paraphrase material from the sources. The sources would not be cross-referenced, or linked to own knowledge and there would be little attempt to answer the question. |
| **Level 2**<br><br>5–9 marks | Comprehends the sources and notes points of challenge and support for the stated claim. Combines the information from the sources to illustrate points linked to the question.<br><br>Low: 5–6 marks, high: 7–9 marks | A level 2 answer will generally use the sources more extensively and points will be picked out from them that agree or disagree with the view presented in the question. It is still likely to be summarising what the sources say. It may work through the sources in sequence, or begin to use the sources in combination. | A level 2 response to the question given above will begin to focus on the question and will use material from the sources to form a very basic for and against structure. There might be some attempt to cross-reference. |
| **Level 3**<br><br>10–14 marks | Interprets the sources with confidence, showing the ability to analyse some key points of the arguments offered and to reason from the evidence of the sources. Develops points of challenge and support for the stated claim from the provided source material and deploys material gained from relevant reading and knowledge of the issues under discussion. Shows clear understanding that the issue is one of interpretation.<br><br>Low: 10–11 marks, high: 12–14 marks | A level 3 answer will show an understanding that the sources present differing interpretations in relation to the view expressed in the question. This is likely to be achieved by examining some of the evidence that agrees with the view in the question and then looking at the evidence that disagrees with it. At level 3 the sources will be used mostly to provide information rather than interpretations. The sources will be cross-referenced. | A typical level 3 response to the same question will use information from the sources thematically. It may contain paragraphs on the key personalities, the economic imbalance or SDI. In so doing it will indicate a clear attempt to answer the question. |

| Level | Level descriptor | Descriptor comments | Example |
|---|---|---|---|
| **Level 4**<br><br>15–19 marks | Interprets the sources with confidence showing the ability to understand the basis of the arguments offered by the authors and to relate these to wider knowledge of the issues under discussion. Discussion of the claim in the question proceeds from an exploration of the issues raised by the process of analysing the sources and the extension of these issues from other relevant reading and own knowledge of the points under debate. Presents an integrated response with developed reasoning and debating of the evidence in order to create judgements in relation to the stated claim, although not all the issues will be fully developed. Reaches and sustains a conclusion based on the discriminating use of the evidence.<br><br>Low: 15–16 marks, high: 17–19 marks | A level 4 answer will focus on the interpretations offered by the sources. These will be linked confidently to the wider debate to which the question refers.<br>The sources will be integrated with one another. The essay will arrive at a judgement based on the interpretations offered by the sources and the evidence from own knowledge. | A level 4 response to the question, using the sources provided, may well begin by addressing the argument of Source 1, the argument to which the question refers. It could link this to Source 2's claim that economic problems were part of the reason for the abandonment of the Brezhnev Doctrine. Students could then link this to own knowledge and explain how the 'New Thinking' reflected Gorbachev's acknowledgement that there were major problems with the Soviet economic model. Later paragraphs could combine sources and own knowledge to address the other issues raised in the sources and reach a judgement. |
| **Level 5**<br><br>20–24 marks | Interprets the sources with confidence and discrimination, assimilating the author's arguments and displaying independence of thought in the ability to assess the presented views in the light of own knowledge and reading. Treatment of argument and discussion of evidence will show that the full demands of the question have been appreciated and addressed. Presents a sustained evaluative argument and reaches fully substantiated conclusions demonstrating an understanding of the nature of historical debate.<br><br>Low: 20–21 marks, high: 22–24 marks | A level 5 answer will focus on the interpretations offered by the sources, assimilating these into an overall argument, focused on the question. Material from the sources will be precisely selected and used with confidence. Level 5 answers will assess the interpretations offered by the sources in the light of their own knowledge. A level 5 answer will address the full demands of the question and reach a fully substantiated conclusion, based on a sustained argument. | In some ways a level 5 response would be similar to a level 4 response. Both would focus on the question, evaluate the interpretations of the sources and integrate the sources with own knowledge to reach a judgement. However, at level 5 the essay would have an overall argument that runs throughout the essay. Finally, the conclusion would flow naturally from the argument contained in the essay. |

### Reaching a developed judgement

Bear in mind that your essay is weighing up an interpretation. Therefore, you will need to reach a judgement regarding that claim as part of your essay. Think carefully about whether you agree or disagree with the claim made in the question. Ideally, you will reach a view before you begin writing the essay and argue your case throughout the essay. Remember, though, that you must take account of the points that *challenge* as well as those that support your case. Remember, too, that you are not *evaluating* the sources, you are using your own knowledge and evidence from other sources to examine the claims that they are making.

The examiner is not looking for a particular answer. Rather, the examiner will be looking at the quality of your argument and the way you use the sources and your own knowledge during your argument.

### Key tips for structuring your answer: dos and don'ts

| Do |
| --- |
| ✓ Read both questions and check that you understand their focus before selecting which to answer. |
| ✓ Plan your answer carefully – use different-coloured pens to indicate sources and own knowledge. |
| ✓ Reach a judgement about how far you agree with the statement in the question before beginning your essay. Develop a clear argument that supports your judgement throughout the essay. |
| ✓ Focus directly on the question throughout your essay. |
| ✓ Examine the sources looking for evidence that: <br>   ✓ supports the claim made in the question <br>   ✓ contradicts the claim made in the question <br>   ✓ offers an alternative interpretation to the one offered in the question. |
| ✓ Cross-reference the sources. |
| ✓ Integrate the sources with your own knowledge throughout the essay. Use your own knowledge to develop interpretations offered by the sources, to counter interpretations offered by the sources and to offer new interpretations. |
| ✓ Make sure your essay reaches a judgement regarding the interpretation offered by the question. Do this by weighing up the interpretations offered by the sources and your own knowledge. |

**Don't**

Begin to write without planning.

✗ Describe what the sources say.

✗ Work through the sources in sequence, without cross-referencing them with one another.

✗ Provide your own knowledge in a separate section of the essay to your discussion of the sources.

✗ Discuss the provenance and reliability of the sources.

✗ Forget to link the points you make to the question you are answering.

✗ Write an essay mainly from your own knowledge, ignoring the sources.

✗ Describe the way historians' views differ over the ending of the Cold War, rather than answering the question that has been set.

Fail to reach a judgement in your conclusion.

## Exemplars and commentaries

### Section A: essay question 1

*'Between 1953 and 1961, US–Soviet relations were based on confrontation rather than co-existence.'*
*How far do you agree with this view?* **[30 marks]**

This essay question requires you to make and justify an historical judgement about the extent to which US–Soviet relations in the stated period were characterised by confrontation rather than co-existence. An examiner will be looking for:

- an analytical (not a descriptive) response, which focuses on US–Soviet relations
- relevant supporting evidence drawn from across the 1953–61 timeframe
- an informed assessment of the 'confrontation' and 'co-existence' viewpoints
- a substantiated judgement that supports or challenges the statement in the question.

### Grade C student answer

Under the post-Stalin collective leadership, a policy of 'peaceful co-existence' was officially adopted, easing tensions. This demonstrated a Soviet readiness to negotiate with the West and provided something of a thaw as ground was conceded in the interest of sustaining peace. One can also argue that the aims of 'peaceful co-existence' were on several occasions undermined by the actions of the USSR, such as the intervention into Hungary in 1956 in order to preserve its territory. Equally, Eisenhower and Dulles maintained a suspicious US stance regarding the actions of the USSR. They showed on numerous occasions that they were prepared to use force if necessary to prevent the further spread of communism.

One could argue that the confrontational undertones of the supposed post-Stalin thaw were epitomised by the actions of Eisenhower and Dulles. For example, at the Geneva Conference 1954, agreement was made whereby France withdrew its troops from Indochina. Dulles walked out of the conference, fearing the agreement had affirmed communism in North Vietnam. In the same year, Eisenhower announced his Domino Theory concerning the spread of communism through Asia. To counter this, Dulles recommended a policy of 'massive atomic ☞

This is not a strong introduction. It attempts to focus on the question and outlines some of the relevant competing arguments but there are several weaknesses too. The paragraph would be improved by incorporating explicit references to the co-existence–confrontation debate, which is central to the question (the key term 'confrontation' is not used at all in the introduction), and by offering an opening judgement on the statement in the question to give a clear and early indication of the case that will be put forward and ending with an explicit link to the question. As it stands, the paragraph is left hanging.

and thermonuclear retaliation', exemplifying an extremely hostile stance towards the USSR. Similarly, in 1957 Eisenhower proposed what is now called the Eisenhower Doctrine, which assured 'armed aggression' in support of any country under the threat of international communism. Echoing the Truman Doctrine 10 years previously, this cemented the US position of hostility towards the Soviet Union and opposition to the spread of communism. In this sense confrontation overrode any notion of co-existence.

Although Malenkov and Khrushchev adopted a policy of 'peaceful co-existence', they also displayed a confrontational stance throughout the period. The Russians employed military force in Hungary to prevent the country leaving the Warsaw Pact and setting up a multi-party political system. This episode, which left the hard-line Kadar in power and 35 000 dead, reveals that although the Soviets endorsed 'peaceful co-existence', they – like the Americans – were willing to use military strength if necessary. Confrontation also surfaced over Berlin in 1961. As West Germany prospered under the control of the capitalist powers, East Germany was stripped bare by the Soviets who were determined to prevent a resurgent Germany. As a result there began an exodus of people from East Germany to the West. Consequently, Khrushchev called for Berlin to become a free city and for the West to officially acknowledge East Germany as a nation. To maintain the Eastern Bloc Khrushchev embarked on a military-style mission literally to cement the Iron Curtain by building a security wall in Berlin. From then on, this became the dividing line between the influence of the USA and Russia. For the USSR too, vital interests meant that confrontation took precedence over co-existence.

However, one could also look at a number of events in the period of 1953–61 where co-existence was at least attempted and achieved a moderate amount of success. Under the collective Soviet leadership, the Russians' grip on Eastern Europe was relaxed. The Austrian State Treaty 1955, for example, saw both powers removing their military presence from the divided Austria and confirming it as a neutral state. Khrushchev saw this treaty as a demonstration to the US that they were willing to make concessions in the interest of peace. Similarly, in 1956 the Soviets withdrew from Finland. Having received the Porkkala region in 1947, by 1955 Khrushchev went against the wishes of Molotov and seeing no tactical ☞

This analytical paragraph shows some understanding of the focus of the question. It develops the confrontation argument by referring relevantly to some aspects of the USA's anti-communist stance in the 1950s. However, this section could be improved by examining the actual impact of the USA's stated position on US–Soviet relations, to give greater depth and development to the analysis. It could also be improved by widening the range of evidence, since all the examples given of US 'confrontation' are drawn from either 1954 or 1957.

This is another analytical paragraph, showing some understanding of the focus of the question. It continues to develop the confrontation argument by referring relevantly, and accurately, to the USSR's uncompromising approach to Hungary and Germany. However, the actual impact of the USSR's actions on US–Soviet relations could be developed further by examining the role of Soviet repression in Hungary in hardening Western attitudes and then analysing (rather than largely describing, as it does here) superpower confrontation over the Berlin issue.

advantages in the Soviet presence – gave Finland back the region. Finland remained largely neutral throughout the remainder of the 1950s and 1960s. In the same way, peace was achieved in Indochina at the Geneva conference in 1954. French forces were removed from the region and Indochina was divided into different states. These treaties showed Soviet willingness to negotiate and even concede some ground to the West in the interests of 'peaceful co-existence'. Similarly, the USSR cut the Red Army by 600 000 troops across the Eastern Bloc, endorsed Yugoslav leader Tito on Khrushchev's 1955 visit and officially recognised West Germany as a state. Perhaps the largest stride in US–Soviet relations came in 1959 when Khrushchev accepted an invitation to visit the USA. To a large extent Khrushchev's visit was a success, with the American public warming to their enemy.

This paragraph moves on to consider the co-existence counterargument – the other vital component of the answer. It gives a wider range of relevant examples to illustrate that superpower co-existence was not an empty concept. This counterargument is clearly set out and the analysis offers some assessment of the impact of key events on US–Soviet relations. This makes it a stronger paragraph than the previous one, but it could be further improved with a final sentence explicitly linking the analysis to the question.

In the period 1953–61 obvious attempts were made to reduce Cold War tensions. The treaties made regarding Austria and Indochina as well as state visits and conferences show that the Soviets, in particular, were willing to make concessions in order to maintain peace. However, all the movements towards peaceful co-existence were undermined by the confrontational attitudes of the US and Soviet regimes. For example, any liberalisation in Eastern Europe by the USSR was undercut by the Soviet brutality in Hungary. Likewise, the 1954 Indochina Conference saw Dulles storm out over the issue and only agree sceptically. Even on Khrushchev's 1959 visit, when denied access to Disneyland on health reasons, he believed it was because the US were hiding rocket launch pads there. Therefore, overall, US–Soviet relations were still based on confrontation, which was symbolised by the construction of the Berlin Wall. ☞

The conclusion is well focused on the question and reaches an overall judgement on the confrontation–co-existence issue.

This is a moderate answer.
- It is analytical, showing understanding of the focus of the question – particularly the need to analyse both the confrontation and co-existence viewpoints.
- There is some evaluation of the argument, as shown, for example, in the conclusion. The answer would be improved by evaluating the strengths and weaknesses of the confrontation and co-existence viewpoints in the main section.
- Mostly accurate and relevant evidence is used
- The argument shows some direction and control but occasionally loses focus. The answer would be improved by a sharper focus on the question in the introduction and in the paragraph on Hungary and Germany.

Overall, this answer achieves **low level 4 and would gain 19 out of 30 marks**.

**Grade A\* student answer**

After Stalin's death in 1953, US–Soviet relations appeared to improve, prompting some commentators to describe the years up to 1961 as a period of superpower co-existence. This 'thaw' in the Cold War, epitomised by the 'Spirit of Geneva' and summit diplomacy, helped to ease US–Soviet tensions but failed to address the key issues (such as ideological differences) that continued to divide the two sides. Indeed, on closer inspection, it seems clear that the US–Soviet relationship remained essentially confrontational during these years, since it was based on conflicting objectives and considerable suspicion. Moreover, in reality, neither America nor the USSR placed much faith in their rival's commitment to peaceful co-existence, which further encouraged both superpowers to take a hard-line stance.

The competing world views championed by the USA and the Soviet Union made confrontation virtually unavoidable and co-existence highly problematic. On the Soviet side, Khrushchev rejected any notion of 'ideological peaceful co-existence'. He was convinced that 'victory will inevitably be ours' in the capitalist–communist struggle because the West's prosperity would eventually be undermined by an economic slump. The Soviet strategy, therefore, was to avoid a nuclear war, exploit favourable opportunities if they arose and wait for the collapse of capitalism. President Eisenhower remained sceptical about co-existence and publicly condemned the USSR as an ideologically hostile power that was 'ruthless in purpose and insidious in method'. Eisenhower's Domino Theory (1954), the Eisenhower Doctrine (1957) and the 'New Look' defence policy (with its emphasis on nuclear deterrence that would deliver 'more bang for your buck') were all formulated to halt the spread of communism in Europe and Asia. In short, both superpowers continued to assume that their relationship would be based on confrontation rather than co-existence.

These attitudes inevitably shaped Cold War politics in the years 1953 to 1961. In part, US–Soviet tension was heightened by the accelerating nuclear arms race of the 1950s, as both nations attempted to establish a technological advantage with the development of the hydrogen bomb and ICBMs. The USA was also particularly concerned that the Soviet Union would seek to expand communist influence in Africa, the Middle East and Asia, as Britain and France abandoned their imperial roles. ☞

This is a highly effective introduction. It is precisely focused on the question and outlines the competing arguments in the co-existence–confrontation debate. It also offers an opening judgement that US–Soviet relations were largely based on confrontation, which gives a clear and early indication of the case that will be put forward. Furthermore, rounding off the introduction with an opening judgement provides an effective route into the main body of the essay, where the detailed analysis will take place.

In terms of knowledge and understanding, this is an impressive paragraph. It offers a sustained analytical focus on the ideological reservations both sides had about meaningful co-existence, including the Soviets' conviction that capitalism would inevitably collapse and the USA's determination to prevent further communist expansion. These important points are effectively reinforced by short quotations from Khrushchev and Eisenhower. The student has taken the trouble to memorise these from mainstream A-level books on the Cold War. Note also how the last sentence ends the paragraph with a clear link to the question.

Certainly, Khrushchev believed that the Third World would opt for communism after decades of colonial and capitalist exploitation. American fears were heightened by the Suez Crisis (1956), which led to the US-backed CENTO Pact of 1958, a Middle East defence alliance. For Eisenhower, CENTO (the Central Treaty Organisation) delivered a clear 'keep out' message to the Soviet Union. In Europe, superpower confrontation centred on the status of Berlin. Khrushchev's attempts to close the city to the West and stem the exodus from East Germany between 1958 and 1961 provoked strong US resistance. At the height of the crisis, in 1961, Kennedy considered a limited nuclear 'first strike' against Soviet military targets. A US–Soviet tank 'stand-off' took place at Checkpoint Charlie and the symbol of enduring East–West hostility, the Berlin Wall, was constructed. In such an atmosphere, each side viewed the actions of the other with intense suspicion. Eisenhower's 'Open Skies' initiative (1955), for instance, was dismissed by Khrushchev as an American plot to 'look inside our bedrooms'. Similarly, the successful *Sputnik* launch (1957) prompted a shocked US to establish NASA (1958), thereby extending the Cold War into space. Thus, throughout this period, US–Soviet relations were dominated by confrontation and brinkmanship.

In one key respect, however, both America and the Soviet Union recognised the advantages of co-existence now that they each possessed nuclear weapons. For all its rhetoric about 'rollback' and 'massive retaliation', the US rejected intervention in East Germany (1953) and Hungary (1956) so as to avoid an almost inevitable nuclear exchange. The American decision was also a tacit recognition that Eastern Europe was a Soviet sphere of influence. Eisenhower also wisely refused to react to the 'missile gap' panic in the US in the late 1950s. On other occasions, the USSR acted as a moderating influence. The new Soviet leadership brokered a peace agreement to end the Korean War (1953) and Khrushchev refused Mao's requests for nuclear weapons during the 1950s in case the 'unrestrained' Chinese communist leader escalated the East–West conflict by using atomic bombs against US interests in south-east Asia. In addition, when the US sponsored and supported coups against 'left-wing' regimes in Iran (1953) and Guatemala (1954), the USSR took no action. Clearly, the ever-present threat of nuclear annihilation provided a powerful motive for US–Soviet co-existence based on the mutual acceptance of spheres of influence. ☞

This paragraph sustains the analytical focus. It develops the confrontation argument by referring relevantly and accurately to several sources of US–Soviet tension. It is particularly pleasing that the examples were drawn from different parts of the world and taken from across the timeframe stated in the question. As a result, this paragraph has range and depth.

The student moves on to consider the co-existence counterargument – the other vital component of the answer. An equally impressive range of examples is used to make the case that superpower co-existence was primarily driven by US and Soviet fears of a nuclear war. This counterargument is clearly set out and confidently analysed. For example, US reluctance to intervene in Hungary in 1956 is used to develop the view that both superpowers recognised the other's sphere of influence and were keen to avoid nuclear war. Once again, the final sentence links the analysis firmly to the question.

To a certain extent too, summit diplomacy encouraged a less confrontational stance and broke down some Cold War barriers. The end of the war in Indochina (1954) and the summits in Geneva (1955) and Camp David (1959) temporarily established friendlier American–Soviet relations and appeared to boost the prospects for superpower co-existence. Anthony Eden, the British Prime Minister, summed up the so-called 'Spirit of Geneva' in 1955 by noting that 'no country attending wanted war and each understood why'. Indeed, a greater readiness to compromise and negotiate over specific issues led to US–USSR scientific exchanges and US–Soviet acceptance of a neutral Austria (1955). Yet there were obvious limits to summit diplomacy. The 'Spirit of Camp David' quickly evaporated in the wake of the U-2 spy plane incident (1960) and the 1961 Kennedy–Khrushchev talks in Vienna stalled over the issue of Berlin. Whenever vital interests appeared to be at stake, co-existence, such as it was, rapidly gave way to confrontation.

This penultimate paragraph maintains the high-quality analysis of its predecessors. It successfully develops the co-existence counterargument by considering how summit diplomacy helped to reduce US–Soviet tension. At the same time, it draws on specific examples to illustrate that there were clear limitations to the 'Spirit of Geneva'.

In reality, US–Soviet relations between 1953 and 1961 were based on attitudes and policies that encouraged confrontation rather than co-existence. Ideological differences, divisions over Germany and the impact of the nuclear arms race intensified suspicion and frequently led to both superpowers adopting a hard-line stance. Having said this, co-existence was not an entirely meaningless concept for either side, particularly when the threat of nuclear escalation or the settlement of 'non-controversial' issues was involved. Ultimately though, the politics of confrontation prevailed because neither superpower accepted the other's objectives and both doubted their rival's commitment to peaceful co-existence.

The conclusion flows naturally from the main analysis and draws together the key arguments set out earlier in the essay. It is firmly focused on the question and reaches an overall judgement on the confrontation–co-existence issue.

This is an excellent answer.

- It is a focused and sustained analysis, culminating in an explicit judgement that convincingly endorses the 'confrontation' argument.
- It shows understanding and evaluation of the key arguments on both sides of the confrontation–co-existence debate.
- It uses accurate and relevant evidence from across the 1953–61 timeframe to support the analysis.

Overall, this answer achieves a **level 5 and would gain the full 30 marks.**

## Section A: essay question 2

*Why did détente fail to end the Cold War in the 1970s?* **[30 marks]**

This essay question requires you to provide a causal analysis of the failure of détente to bring the Cold War to an end in the 1970s. An examiner will be looking for:

- an analytical (not a descriptive) response, which focuses on the relevant developments during détente
- appropriate supporting evidence drawn from across the 1970s timeframe
- an informed assessment of the causes of failure
- a substantiated judgement on the relative importance of these causes.

### Grade C student answer

The Cold War can be defined as a state of extreme tension (short of outright war) between the USA and the USSR. Both were attempting to become the dominant superpower and their rivalry was based on conflicting ideologies – capitalism and communism. One manifestation of this was the US–Soviet nuclear arms race, which brought the world to the edge of destruction during the Cuban Missile Crisis of October 1962. This 'close call' led to the introduction of superpower détente that aimed to ease hostility between the USSR and the USA. It was introduced as a conscious effort to improve superpower relations and slow down the US–Soviet arms race. This relaxation of tensions was brought to a halt by the Soviet invasion of Afghanistan in 1979, although détente had been deteriorating for some time before this event. Détente failed to end the Cold War for a number of different reasons, yet underlying all of these were the conflicting ideologies of the USA and USSR.

Initially, the state of international relations aided the process of détente. The USSR was willing to work more constructively with the USA because the Soviets were threatened by the rising power of China. However, there was continuing tension between the USA and the USSR over global expansion and the spread of competing ideologies. Soviet and Cuban involvement in the Angolan Civil War in 1975, as well as further interventions in other African states including Mozambique and ☞

This is not a strong introduction. On the plus side, it offers a basic definition of détente and puts forward an initial judgement at the end. However, much of the opening paragraph dwells on the general historical context leading up to détente. It could be improved with more focus on the causal factors that lie at the heart of the question. There are only brief references to 'different reasons' and 'conflicting ideologies'.

Ethiopia, was viewed by the US as evidence of continuing communist expansion. In response, Carter increased arms supplies to anti-communist groups in the developing world in countries such as El Salvador and Nicaragua in order to contain Soviet influence. Essentially, the two superpowers continued their extreme state of tension through war by proxy. The final breaking point was the Soviet invasion of Afghanistan in 1979, which the Americans regarded as evidence of ongoing communist expansion. In their view, the Soviet leadership simply exploited détente to gain advantages for the USSR.

This broadly analytical paragraph shows some understanding of the focus of the question. It develops the argument by referring relevantly to some aspects of the continued superpower Cold War competition in the 1970s. It also establishes a link to the question by connecting 'war by proxy' to a continued 'state of tension'. Nevertheless, the paragraph neither starts nor finishes with an explicit link to the question.

The 1975 Helsinki Accords, which were signed by both the USA and the USSR, appeared to be evidence of the success of détente in promoting human rights. However, when Carter was elected to the Presidency in 1976 he attempted to connect détente to the progress of human rights in the USSR. He hoped that this foreign policy would reduce tension between the two superpowers but in fact the USA's emphasis on human rights did the reverse and actually increased tension. Détente weakened when the Soviet Union violated human rights agreements that it had signed in Helsinki. In the USSR, there was unease in the *Politburo* over the criticisms from the West regarding the Helsinki Accords.

Another broadly analytical paragraph, showing some understanding of the focus of the question. It continues to develop the argument by considering the issue of human rights but the analysis requires more detailed evidence to support the case being made. Once again, the paragraph would be improved by starting or finishing with an explicit link to the question.

The success of détente was always dependent on the willingness of the political leaders to work together. Under President Nixon and Henry Kissinger (his advisor on National Security Affairs), US cooperation with Brezhnev appeared to show a genuine willingness to improve relations based on a constructive approach and mutual respect. This closeness was never repeated after Nixon's departure and as Brezhnev's health continued to deteriorate. Under President Carter, criticism of détente increased as America regained confidence after the Vietnam War. A movement arose in the USA who condemned détente as being too soft on communism and encouraged a need for a more forceful approach to the Soviet Union. These critics promoted the need to resume the arms race in order to exploit the USA's technological and economic superiority over the USSR. This criticism had a big influence on Carter's foreign policy decisions. Similar opposition had also emerged in the USSR. In particular, pressure was exerted by the Soviet military to resume the arms race to ensure its position against America. ☞

This paragraph moves on to consider the influence of anti-détente factions in the USA and the USSR. It incorporates relevant examples (for example, the Soviet military) but would be improved by the inclusion of more development of the argument. Moreover, the links to the question need to be made more explicit by clearly connecting the deteriorating Carter–Brezhnev relationship and group opposition to the failure to end the Cold War.

One element of détente was the SALT treaties in 1972 and 1979, which were supposed to deliver a restriction on arms. Although the treaties lessened the arms race they never stopped it. SALT I was largely ineffective as, although it limited the number of missiles, it did not tackle the MIRV issue. In 1973 the USA had 6000 warheads and the USSR had only 2000. By 1977 the USA held 10000 and the USSR 4000. Neither country was prepared to stop their plans for global domination and being ahead in the arms race. Furthermore, neither the USA nor the USSR considered ending their reliance on nuclear weapons and so the threat of nuclear weapons was still evident during the period of détente. SALT II was expected to impose tighter restrictions, yet these were never ratified due to rising tensions.

This penultimate paragraph examines the role of another relevant factor – the SALT treaties. The student deploys knowledge of some of the terms of the agreements to illustrate how neither superpower was prepared to end the arms race under détente. However, yet again, the links to the question need to be made more explicit by relating the deficiencies of the SALT treaties and superpower attitudes to the arms race to the failure to end the Cold War. The paragraph would also be strengthened by considering SALT II in more detail.

In conclusion, détente resulted in some benefits as it did dramatically slow down the spiralling arms race. However, this needs to be considered in the context that either country could still obliterate the other and the rest of the world. Fundamentally, détente failed as neither country abandoned its ideological beliefs and expansionist aims.

The conclusion lacks focus on the question and does not properly address the 'failure to end the Cold War' issue. To achieve a higher level, it might also give an indication of the relative importance of the factors discussed in the main part.

This is a moderate answer with significant room for improvement.

- It is broadly analytical, showing some understanding of the focus of the question by concentrating on continued superpower competition, human rights issues, anti-détente factions on both sides, and the weaknesses of the arms limitations agreements.
- Some of the material included is descriptive or only implicitly relevant, such as the opening section of the introduction.
- Accurate and relevant evidence is used but this does not consistently display depth, as the brief reference to SALT II and the section on human rights illustrate.
- The argument shows some direction and control but is not sustained, particularly in the sections on human rights and the leaders.

Overall, this answer achieves a **high level 3 and would gain 18 out of 30 marks.**

**Grade A student answer**

Détente is best defined as the relaxation of tensions between countries. The term is usually applied to US–Soviet relations during the 1970s in the context of the Cold War. Although this period witnessed more constructive superpower engagement, for a number of reasons détente failed to end the Cold War. In particular, the shortcomings of the arms limitations treaties, the friction created by human rights issues, and superpower rivalry in the Third World all ensured that US–Soviet relations continued to be shaped by Cold War competition and mistrust.

Firstly, the SALT I (1972) and SALT II (1979) treaties did not halt the US–Soviet nuclear arms race, which was central to East–West Cold War rivalry. SALT I was the product of superpower negotiation and could boast some real achievements, such as the limited deployment of ABMs (two sites on each side) and a freeze in the number of ICBMs and SLBMs. Nevertheless, the treaty had a number of weaknesses and limitations. The deployment of MIRVs was not prohibited and there was no ban on anti-satellite weapons or restriction on long-range bombers. Consequently, the USA preserved its superiority in terms of deliverable nuclear warheads – about 5700 to 2500 – just as President Nixon intended. In addition, the Basic Agreement (setting out a 'code of conduct' for future superpower relations), which was endorsed by Brezhnev and Nixon, was vaguely worded and proved to be unenforceable. SALT I placed few limits on the US and Soviet nuclear arsenals, both of which continued to expand, and the treaty lasted for just five years. Similarly, SALT II, although it limited both sides to 2400 launchers, lagged behind current technology and left both sides free to continue building nuclear warheads. It also did nothing to prevent the deployment of SS 20, Pershing II and cruise missiles. In any case, crises over the Soviet combat brigade in Cuba and the USSR's invasion of Afghanistan meant that SALT II was never ratified by the US Senate.

Secondly, US–Soviet relations deteriorated over the issue of human rights. Basket 3 of the Helsinki Accords (1975), which were signed by the US and the USSR, committed the signatories to respect human rights (notably freedom of speech, protest and movement). The Soviets only accepted this because the Accords also confirmed the post-war division of Europe and offered important trade agreements. They also thought   ☞

This reasonably effective introduction is focused on the question. It outlines three key reasons why détente failed to end the Cold War. It also provides a definition of the key term. Nevertheless, the student could improve this opening paragraph by offering an initial judgement about the relative importance of these causes. Rounding off the introduction with an initial judgement provides an effective route into the main body of the essay where the detailed analysis will take place.

In terms of knowledge and understanding, this is a good paragraph. The student offers a developed analysis of SALT I and SALT II's failure to end the superpower arms race, based on relevant knowledge of both agreements. Some evaluation of the treaties' lack of impact is also included. Furthermore, the opening sentence clearly links the paragraph to the question. It would have been helpful to conclude this section with a comment about the USA and USSR's reluctance to give too much away in these treaties. This would have provided an effective link back to the question at the end.

that they could 'contain' the human rights issue in the Eastern Bloc. However, encouraged by the Helsinki Accords, Soviet and East European dissidents (including Andrei Sakharov, Vaclav Havel and Alexander Solzhenitsyn) criticised human rights abuses under communist rule. Furthermore, Helsinki 'watch' committees and Charter 77 were set up to check Soviet compliance. The USSR feared that such freedoms would undermine communist Europe and responded with repression. Dissidents were harassed, imprisoned or exiled and some were sent to mental institutions. Soviet Jews were denied the right to emigrate to the USA or Israel. These breaches of the Accords provoked outrage in the West. President Carter attempted to put pressure on the USSR by linking further progress under détente to improvements in the Soviet human rights record. The US Congress also passed the Jackson–Vanik Amendment (1975), which cut American trade with the USSR because of restricted Jewish emigration rights. For their part, the Soviet leadership regarded the handling of the human rights issue as an internal affair and deeply resented what they saw as Western 'interference'.

Finally, it is important to recognise that Cold War conflict and competition for influence continued throughout the 1970s, particularly in the Third World. Indeed, Brezhnev distinguished between détente and the broader attempt to advance the communist cause. He regarded the Third World as a legitimate area for Soviet attempts to develop client states and he was determined to keep this strategy separate from arms control. These interventions heightened US–Soviet tension. Many in the West concluded that the USSR was still aggressively expansionist and disregarding the principles of détente. In 1975, for example, Soviet and Cuban military involvement in the Angolan Civil War enabled the MPLA to take power. Similar Soviet–Cuban ventures later took place in Mozambique, Somalia and Ethiopia. Ultimately, the Soviet invasion of Afghanistan (1979) destroyed détente and, with it, any hope that the Cold War would end. The USSR intervened to maintain a neighbouring pro-Soviet regime in power and prevent the spread of Islamic fundamentalism in the wake of the Iranian revolution (1978–9). America viewed the Soviet occupation as part of a wider plan to dominate the Persian Gulf and cut off oil supplies to the West. ☞

This paragraph develops the argument by referring relevantly and accurately to growing US–Soviet tension over the issue of human rights. Once again, several key examples are discussed. However, throughout the paragraph, the links to the question are implicit, not explicit. Neither the opening nor the concluding sentence comments specifically on détente's failure to end the Cold War. This is a shame because the analysis has range and depth but should be more clearly connected to the question.

This penultimate paragraph resembles the one before. It continues to develop the argument by considering the impact of superpower rivalry in the Third World, which culminated in the 1979 Soviet invasion of Afghanistan. There is also some evaluation of the impact of continued superpower competition. As before, a range of relevant evidence is used but stronger links to the question are needed. The opening sentence makes only an implicit reference to the question and the final statement is not explicitly connected to détente's failure to end the Cold War.

In conclusion, détente failed to end the Cold War for three key reasons. First, neither the US nor the USSR were prepared to make important concessions during the SALT I and SALT II negotiations to halt the arms race. Second, the issue of human rights increased East–West tensions due to the impact of the Helsinki Accords. Finally, although détente was intended to improve US–Soviet relations, superpower competition for influence in the Third World continued throughout the 1970s.

The conclusion is linked to the question and the earlier analysis, but does little more than summarise the three reasons discussed in the main section. A stronger conclusion would have reached a judgement on the relative importance of the three factors identified in the essay.

This is a good answer with the qualities of a mid-level 4 response.

- The analytical response mostly relates well to the focus of the question and shows some understanding of the key issues relating to détente (for example, SALT, the Helsinki Accords, and superpower involvement in the Third World).
- There is some evaluation of the key arguments, such as the shortcomings of the arms limitations agreements, US–Soviet friction over human rights and continued Cold War rivalries in the Third World.
- It uses accurate and relevant evidence to support the analysis in all three selected areas.
- However, this answer would be improved by ensuring that explicit links to the question are made in each paragraph, and that the conclusion reaches a clear judgement about the relative importance of the causal factors analysed in the main section of the essay.

Overall, this answer achieves **mid-level 4 and would gain 22 out of 30 marks.**

## Section B: controversy question 1

*How far do you agree that the development of the Cold War between 1945 and 1953 was primarily due to ideological divisions?*

*Explain your answer, using the evidence of Sources 1, 2 and 3 and your own knowledge of the issues related to this controversy.* [**40 marks**]

### Source 1

(From an article by Arthur M. Schlesinger Jr, *Origins of the Cold War*, published by the Council on Foreign Relations 1967)

An analysis of the origins of the Cold War, which leaves out three factors – Leninist ideology, the sinister dynamics of a totalitarian society and the madness of Stalin – is obviously incomplete. It was these factors, which made it hard for the West to accept the idea that Russia was moved only by desire to protect its security and would only be satisfied by the control of Eastern Europe. Leninism and totalitarianism created a structure of thought and behaviour, which made post-war collaboration between Russia and America – in any normal sense of civilised relations between national states – impossible.

### Source 2

(From Vojtech Mastny, *The Cold War and Soviet Insecurity*, published by Oxford University Press 1996)

Stalin mistakenly persisted in his belief that Germany could be united on the foundations established in the eastern part of it that he controlled. Admittedly, the German question would have taxed the skill of any Russian statesman. More important than the magnitude of Stalin's problems, however, was his tendency to pile them up and make them worse by bungling. Such blunders as the Berlin blockade or the row with Tito would have been sufficient for Stalin to be sacked if he had been the head of a responsible government. Since he was not, he could afford to merely cut his losses and proceed with more blunders – none greater than his lending support to Kim Il-Sung's adventure in Korea.

### Source 3

(From Martin McCauley, *Origins of the Cold War 1941–49*, published by Longman 2008)

Stalin must bear much of the blame for the Cold War because he had it within his power in 1945 to fashion a working relationship with the United States. Neither Stalin nor Truman wanted a Cold War. Perhaps in 1945 both the Soviet and American leaders were too confident that their own system would eventually win. However, in the shorter term, because of the destruction of war, both felt nervous about the other's ability to steal a march on them. Stalin, although essentially a practical politician, was also influenced by Marxism. This held that an understanding with capitalist opponents would be transitory but useful until the next capitalist crisis broke out. This would place the Soviet Union in a good position to take maximum advantage of it.

This controversy question requires you to make and justify an historical judgement about the extent to which the development of the Cold War between 1945 and 1953 was primarily due to ideological divisions. An examiner will be looking for:

- an analytical (not a descriptive) response, focusing on the competing interpretations of the development of the Cold War (1945–53) and evaluating them
- relevant supporting evidence drawn from the sources provided and your own knowledge
- effective cross-referencing of the source material to develop a support/challenge approach
- effective integration of the source material and your own knowledge
- a conclusion containing a substantiated judgement that supports or challenges the statement in the question.

### Grade C student answer

Many factors contributed to the development of the Cold War. Ideological differences between capitalism and communism were perhaps most significant, as these led to a fundamental division between the two powers. There were others too, including the clash of the Cold War leaders' personalities, Soviet expansionism (particularly in Eastern Europe) and misunderstanding, which often created more tension.

Competing ideologies played a big role in the origins of the Cold War. Source 1 talks of the Soviet Union in terms of 'Leninist ideology' and a 'totalitarian society', features that the capitalist USA strongly opposed. This created tension between the superpowers. Source 3 also indicates how the USSR was locked in a long-term struggle with its 'capitalist opponents'. Ideological differences also led to the division of Europe. The formation of NATO in 1949 excluded Russia, leaving them isolated and feeling vulnerable. Eventually the Warsaw Pact was formed by the USSR in 1955 to protect the communist movement. Furthermore, the USA needed more markets in Europe, which led to the 'Open Door' policy, free trade and the Marshall Plan 1947, which offered aid to all European countries to help rebuild their economies. However, the conditions attached made it impossible for the Soviet Bloc to accept. In addition, the USSR saw this not as an altruistic act but as US neo-imperialism. Indeed, Molotov accused America of 'dollar-imperialism', as the Soviets believed America was using capitalist methods to strengthen its influence abroad. These things ☞

This is a fairly basic introduction. On the plus side, it offers several reasons for the development of the Cold War and appears to make a provisional judgement regarding the importance of ideological divisions. However, this opening paragraph would be improved by briefly linking the sources provided to these causes and rounding off with an explicit link to the question.

This paragraph is broadly analytical and shows some understanding of the focus of the question. It develops the argument by partially cross-referencing Sources 1 and 3 and then integrates the student's own knowledge to add range and depth. Nevertheless, several improvements could be made, such as incorporating additional relevant material from Sources 1 and 3 (for example, Source 3 points out that Stalin was 'influenced by Marxism' and Source 1 refers to the 'structure of thought and behaviour' created by Leninism and totalitarianism), using information from Source 2 (for example, Stalin's wish to establish a united communist Germany), offering a critical evaluation of the 'ideological divisions' argument and ending with a more convincing link to the question.

created great mistrust and differences between the US and the USSR and led to poor relations. Therefore ideological differences influenced the Cold War.

The personalities of the post-war leaders also influenced the origins of the Cold War. Source 1 talks of the 'madness of Stalin' and this is illustrated by Source 2, which talks about a number of foreign policy 'blunders' such as the 'Berlin Blockade', the 'row with Tito' and supporting the 'Kim Il-Sung's adventure in Korea'. Furthermore, Stalin showed disregard for the allies because he did not hold free elections. However, Stalin was not the only post-war leader to cause bad relations. Source 3 agrees by suggesting that Stalin and Truman failed to build post-war peace as they were 'too confident that their own system would eventually win'. Truman took a number of actions that created mistrust between him and Stalin. He failed to let Stalin know about the bombing of Hiroshima in August 1945, and cut off lend-lease to the USSR abruptly. Truman had been thrust into the position of President following the death of Roosevelt. He was very inexperienced in negotiation and this can be seen by his upbraiding of Molotov. Thus, the foreign policy failures of Stalin and the inexperience of Truman created a climate of mistrust and rivalry.

Sources 1 and 2 agree that Soviet expansionism was a major cause of the Cold War. Source 1 states that the Soviets 'would only be satisfied by the control of Eastern Europe' and Source 2 alludes to Stalin's belief that 'Germany could be united on the foundations established in the eastern part of it that he controlled'. This shows the Soviet Union's clear desire to expand its influence across Europe – as seen by the establishment of the COMINFORM (1947) and COMECON (1949), and the imposition of the Berlin Blockade (1948–9) in an attempt to force the West out of Berlin. The USSR also supported Kim Il-Sung in the Korean War to expand into Asia. However, there is a lot of evidence to suggest that the Soviet Union was not expansionist. The post-war economic condition of the USSR meant it was in no position to act aggressively. Soviet wartime losses amounted to 19% of its pre-war population. Stalin also refused to support the communists in the Greek Civil War and he did not object to the US presence in South Korea. Therefore it is inconclusive whether Soviet expansionism was a major factor in causing the Cold War.

Misunderstandings and perceptions were another factor in the Cold War. Stalin was suspicious of delays ☞

This is another broadly analytical paragraph that again shows some understanding of the focus of the question. It continues to develop the argument by considering the impact of the leaders. All three sources are cross-referenced to build the case and the student's own knowledge gives some added depth to the analysis of Truman's role. Having said this, although Stalin's 'blunders' are mentioned, they need to be explained to develop the argument. An evaluation of this 'personality' viewpoint should be included and the paragraph requires explicit links to the question.

This paragraph moves on to consider the role of Soviet expansionism in the development of the Cold War. Sources 1 and 2 are cross-referenced relevantly and the student incorporates some relevant examples to reinforce the argument. Some evaluation of this view is also attempted.

In terms of essay structure, it would have been more effective to include this analysis in the 'ideological divisions' section because of its obvious links with communist 'global' objectives. Once again, the links to the question should be made explicit.

in launching the second front and believed that the West was delaying to weaken the USSR. Furthermore, at Yalta the Russians assumed that the Western powers had given them a free hand in Eastern Europe whereas Britain and the US believed they had a Soviet pledge to hold free elections. Furthermore, the Stalinisation of Europe was a defensive act but America saw it as expansionist. Perhaps this was due to geographical reasons, as the USA was not able to sympathise with the Soviet fear of invasion. Similarly, US aid to Europe through the Marshall Plan (which amounted to $13 billion in total) was altruistic but the Soviets saw it as aggressive or 'dollar imperialism'. Therefore, it is clear that misunderstanding played a role in the origins of the Cold War.

In conclusion, although there is evidence to suggest that Soviet expansionism had an impact on the origins of the Cold War, there is a lot of conflicting evidence that suggests this is not the most important factor. While the superpowers' misunderstandings and the major personalities caused friction and mistrust, leading to poor relations, the most important reason was ideological differences. Capitalism and communism are polarised, meaning both the USSR and the USA had little understanding and respect for each other's system. This, ultimately, was the most important factor in causing the Cold War.

The major weakness of this paragraph is that it makes no reference to the extracts provided, when Sources 1 and 3 both contain relevant material on the 'misjudgement' viewpoint. For example, Source 1 refers to Western doubts about Soviet security motives and Source 3 considers that both sides were 'too confident' but also 'nervous' about each other. Such material should be included here. Instead, the student offers some relevant own knowledge but with limited range and depth. Links to the question should be made more explicit and an evaluation of this argument should also be included to improve the link of the paragraph.

The conclusion is linked to the question and reaches a judgement about the relative importance of ideological divisions. Nevertheless, this final statement would have carried more conviction if Soviet expansionism had been incorporated into the overall 'ideological divisions' argument.

This moderate answer contains the qualities of a level 3 response in AO1 and AO2.

- It shows ability to analyse some key points of the arguments offered in the source material, such as capitalist–communist rivalry and the role of Truman and Stalin.
- It reaches a judgement supported by information from the sources and student's own knowledge to attach particular importance to ideological differences.
- It develops some points of support and challenge for the statement in the question by considering ideological divisions, Soviet expansionism, the actions of key personalities and the role of misunderstanding/perception.
- It offers a broadly analytical response from the student's own knowledge that supports the source material.
- It includes generally accurate factual material, drawn from across the 1945–53 timeframe.
- The argument shows some direction and control but is not sustained; for example, the paragraph on misunderstanding/perception lacks explicit links to the question.
- The answer would be improved by ensuring that you have used all the relevant information contained in the sources in the analysis, by evaluating each major argument, and by making sure that every paragraph has clear links to the question.

Overall, this answer achieves **high level 3 for both Assessment Objectives and would gain 23 out of 40 marks (10 for AO1a and b, 13 for AO2b).**

### Grade A* student answer

The reasons for the development of the Cold War (1945–53) have been debated for many years. Historians such as Schlesinger (Source 1) have argued that ideologically-driven Soviet expansionism was the primary cause of rising East–West tension. This interpretation is challenged by Mastny and McCauley (Source 2 and Source 3) who emphasise Stalin's mistakes and the superpowers' perceptions. Collectively, the three sources identify central elements in the historical debate and suggest that deteriorating relations cannot be attributed primarily to ideological divisions. Rather, superpower perceptions, assumptions and misjudgements played the most important role.

Source 1 supports the statement in the question. According to Schlesinger, 'Leninism and totalitarianism', major influences on Soviet foreign policy, established 'a pattern of thought and behaviour', which made normal relations with USA 'impossible'. The other two extracts also offer some backing for the 'ideological divisions' view. Mastny (Source 2) refers to Stalin's belief that a united Germany could be based on the communist 'foundations' of the Soviet sector. Similarly, McCauley (Source 3) argues that the US and Soviet leaders 'were too confident that their own system would eventually win'. From this perspective, a US–Soviet ideological clash produced the Cold War. Russia's commitment to communism (based on Soviet authoritarianism and an ideological mission to impose Marxism globally) brought the USSR into conflict with a USA that was determined to extend free trade, liberal democracy and capitalist economics. Thus, 'influenced by Marxism' (Source 3), Stalin 'communised' Eastern Europe (1945–9), established the COMINFORM (1947) and Comecon (1949), imposed the Berlin Blockade (1948–9) and encouraged communist North Korea to attack South Korea (1950). US actions during the same period were equally ideological – the 'Open Door' policy from 1945, the Truman Doctrine (1947) against 'totalitarianism', and the 'dollar imperialism' of the Marshall Plan (1948). Although capitalist–communist differences clearly played a role in the development of the Cold War, ultimately the 'ideological divisions' argument is too simplistic. It underestimates two related issues discussed in the other extracts: the role of key personalities and each superpower's perceptions of its rival. ☞

This is a strong introduction. It is precisely focused on the question and outlines the competing arguments by briefly referring to all the sources provided. It also offers an opening judgement, which gives a clear and early indication of the case that will be put forward. Furthermore, finishing the introduction with an opening judgement provides an effective route into the main body of the essay where the detailed analysis will take place.

This is a well-constructed and precisely focused paragraph. At the start, extensive cross-referencing of the sources develops the 'ideological divisions' argument. The student has identified elements in all three sources that support the 'ideological' viewpoint. Note too, how short quotations from the extracts are used effectively to build the case. The student's own detailed knowledge is then incorporated to add range and depth to the source-based analysis. Both communist and capitalist ideologies are considered. At the end, the 'ideological divisions' interpretation is critically evaluated, which provides a clear link to the question and moves the analysis smoothly on to the next paragraph.

Collectively, Sources 2 and 3 challenge the 'ideological' viewpoint by offering a more personality-based explanation. Mastny attributes East–West tension to Stalin's tendency to 'pile … up' problems, such as the Berlin Blockade and Korea, and 'make them worse by bungling'. McCauley similarly maintains Stalin 'must bear much of the blame' for the failure to reach a US–Soviet agreement. Even Schlesinger concedes that Stalin's 'madness' played a significant role. Indeed, some of Stalin's policies were ill-conceived and merely sharpened Cold War divisions. The Berlin Blockade 'blunder', for example, led to the creation of West Germany and NATO. Furthermore, Stalin's support for North Korea's aggression in 1950 failed to recognise the USA's determination to defend South Korea. US leaders also affected the development of the Cold War. Roosevelt's death in 1945 marked a turning point because it removed the Western leader who had been flexible enough to establish a constructive wartime working relationship with Stalin up to Yalta (February 1945). Truman, lacking Roosevelt's political stature and experience, adopted a more confrontational approach to the USSR (the 'Iron Fist' policy), partly because he was insecure and keen to establish a strong international reputation. In addition, Source 3 challenges the 'ideological' view by pointing out some of Stalin's decisions aimed to promote 'understanding with capitalist opponents'. Certainly his post-war refusal to assist the Greek communists and his ambivalent attitude to their French and Italian counterparts hardly fit the conventional 'ideological' argument. Once again though, the personality-based case has limitations. It tends to exaggerate the role of individuals and underplays the impact of structural factors, such as political ideologies. In fact, the personalities of the US and Soviet leaders operated under the influence of ideological convictions. This, in turn, led them to make inaccurate assumptions and misjudgements about their superpower rival. Such misperception was the key reason for the development of the Cold War.

A closer reading of the extracts offers a more nuanced explanation for the deterioration in East–West relations. As both Schlesinger and McCauley imply, the US and the USSR found it increasingly difficult to trust each other and suspected their rival's motives. According to Source 1, the West was sceptical that the USSR ☞

This paragraph sustains the high-quality analytical focus. It develops the argument by challenging the 'ideological' view with a personality-based explanation. As before, the sources are cross-referenced effectively to establish the case and extensive own knowledge is then deployed to reinforce the points taken from the extracts. The sources are used in a discriminating way to show that Schlesinger can support the personality view ('madness of Stalin') and McCauley's reference to Stalin's pragmatism can undermine the 'ideological' argument. The evaluation at the end offers a critical appraisal of the personality-based approach and, by linking the latter to ideological factors, introduces the misperception viewpoint.

was 'moved only by desire to protect its security' and concluded that Stalin had an expansionist agenda. Source 3 makes a similar point when it states that 'both felt nervous about the other's ability to steal a march on them'. Indeed, the Truman Doctrine exaggerated the global communist threat partly because the USA incorrectly assumed that the USSR was supporting the communists during the Greek Civil War. Before 1949 too, American refusal to share nuclear technology only increased the Soviets' sense of vulnerability. Moreover, since the USA emerged from the war economically and militarily intact, the Americans did not properly appreciate Russia's urgent need for financial aid and Stalin's determination to achieve Soviet security in Europe after the anti-communist invasions of 1918 and 1941. This encouraged the US to assume that Soviet foreign policy was driven by an expansionist communist ideology rather than limited and defensive national security needs. Furthermore, Stalin's decision to lend 'support to Kim Il-Sung's adventure in Korea' (Source 2) revealed misjudgements on both sides, which heightened Cold War tension. Prior to the war, the Truman administration may have given the North Korean, Chinese and Soviet regimes the false impression that the USA had effectively 'written off' Korea. For its part, the US government erroneously concluded that Stalin had deliberately engineered the Korean War but Truman was unaware of the complex diplomacy between the Soviet leader, Kim Il-Sung and Mao, which preceded the conflict. In short, superpower assumptions, perceptions and misjudgements (generated by various factors including national ideologies and leaders' personalities) produced the Cold War.

In conclusion, rising East–West tension between 1945 and 1953 was not caused primarily by ideological divisions. The sources indicate that such an interpretation is overly simplistic because it fails to examine properly the complex set of assumptions and perceptions, which shaped the deteriorating US–Soviet relationship. ☞

This penultimate paragraph examines the misperception interpretation, using the same combination of confident use of sources, the incorporation of relevant own knowledge and effective evaluation. A particular strength here is the use of different examples to show how misjudgement and misperception lay at the heart of important early Cold War developments (for example, the Soviet pursuit of security in Europe and the Korean War).

The conclusion flows naturally from the main analysis and draws together the key arguments set out earlier in the essay. It is firmly focused on the question and reaches an overall judgement on the 'ideological divisions' argument.

However, this process was, of course, partly influenced by the superpowers' ideological stance and the leaders' personalities. The USA and the USSR increasingly regarded each other's actions as hostile and responded on this basis. To America, Stalin's quest for security was a thinly veiled programme of global communist expansion, which had to be halted. In turn, US efforts to rebuild the shattered European economies and pursue 'Open Door' policies were regarded by the USSR as attempted capitalist penetration of Soviet interests. It was this interaction of flawed assumptions, rather than ideological divisions, which caused the Cold War.

This is an excellent answer with all the qualities of a high level 5 response in AO1 and AO2.

- It interprets the sources with confidence and discrimination, clearly recognising that all three extracts can be used to support different interpretations of the development of the Cold War.
- It presents a sustained evaluative argument regarding the onset of East–West tension.
- It reaches a fully substantiated conclusion that presents a convincing case for the assumption/perception viewpoint.
- Student's own knowledge supports and is integrated with the analysis of the presented source material; this is revealed, for example, in the paragraphs on ideological divisions and the role of key personalities.
- Student's own knowledge is accurate, relevant and demonstrates range and depth across the 1945–53 timeframe.

Overall, this answer achieves **top level 5 for both Assessment Objectives and would gain the full 40 marks (16 for AO1a and b, 24 for AO2b).**

### Section B: controversy question 2

*How far do you agree that the Cold War came to an end in the 1980s due to the USA's economic superiority?*

*Explain your answer, using the evidence of Sources 1, 2 and 3 and your own knowledge of the issues related to this controversy.* **[40 marks]**

### Source 1

(From Eric Hobsbawm, *Age of Extremes: The Short Twentieth Century 1914–1991*, published by Michael Joseph 1994)

Both superpowers overstretched and distorted their economies by a massive and enormously expensive competitive arms race, but the capitalist system could absorb the 3 trillion dollars of debt – essentially for military spending – into which the 1980s plunged the USA. There was nobody to take the equivalent strain on Soviet expenditure, which, in any case, represented a far higher proportion of Soviet production (perhaps 25%) than the 7% of the enormous US GDP* which went on the military in the mid-1980s. Furthermore, the Soviets' allies and dependents never walked on their own feet. They remained a constant and vast annual drain of tens of billions of dollars on the USSR. As for technology, as Western superiority grew dramatically, there was no contest.

*\*GDP stands for Gross Domestic Product – the total value of all the goods and services produced by a nation in one year.*

### Source 2

(From John Lewis Gaddis, *The Cold War*, published by Penguin 2005)

For Gorbachev, any attempt to maintain control over unwilling peoples through the use of force would degrade the Soviet system by overstretching its resources, discrediting its ideology, and resisting the irresistible forces of democratisation that were sweeping the world. He announced to the United Nations General Assembly, on 7 December 1988, that the Soviet Union would unilaterally cut its ground force commitment to the Warsaw Pact by half a million men. It suddenly became apparent, just as Reagan was leaving office, that the Reagan Doctrine had been pushing against an open door. But Gorbachev had also made it clear, to the peoples and the governments of Eastern Europe, that the door was now open.

### Source 3

(From Michael Burleigh, *Sacred Causes: Religion and Politics from the European Dictators to Al Qaeda*, published by HarperPress 2006)

Reagan restored a moral tone to international affairs, most memorably when in March 1983 he referred to the USSR as the 'evil empire'. While that led the Soviets to imagine that they were dealing with a US president crazed enough to launch the bomb, in fact Reagan had a horror of nuclear weapons, and consistently urged on the Soviets the need to remove them through effective anti-ballistic missile defences. That offer in the form of the Strategic Defence Initiative (for deterrence had relied on the absence of just these systems) unlocked the Cold War by denying its permanence and forcing the Russians to realise that they could never compete with America in the most advanced computer and laser technologies.

This controversy question requires you to make and justify an historical judgement about the extent to which the USA's economic superiority was responsible for ending the Cold War in the 1980s. An examiner will be looking for:

- an analytical (not a descriptive) response, which focuses on the competing explanations for the end of the Cold War and evaluates them
- relevant supporting evidence drawn from the sources provided and your own knowledge
- effective cross-referencing of the source material to develop a support/challenge approach
- effective integration of the source material and your own knowledge
- a conclusion containing a substantiated judgement, which supports or challenges the statement in the question.

### Grade C student answer

The role of American economic superiority was highly important in ending the Cold War. However some have questioned the 'triumphalist' approach and have suggested it was the personalities of either Reagan or Gorbachev that led to the end of East–West conflict. Finally, it can be seen that the liberation of Eastern Europe through 'people power' undermined Soviet control over the satellite states and brought the Cold War to a close.

Source 1 points to American economic superiority because, financially, the Soviets' satellite states and allies 'never walked on their own feet' and acted 'as a constant and vast annual drain' on the USSR. Source 2 concurs by stating that Soviet support for its satellites was 'overstretching its resources'. Maintaining these states cost the USSR $40 billion per year, which acted as a significant burden on the Soviet economy. Furthermore, as Source 1 notes, the capitalist system was capable of absorbing trillions of dollars of US debt and American military spending increased to 7% of GDP. The USSR's smaller and less productive economy had to spend 25% of its GDP on military commitments because it could not absorb the 'equivalent strain' in the same way. America was able to commit more funds to the arms race at a time when the USSR economy was flagging. In 1981 the Senate granted an increase of 53% to the military budget, thus giving America a significant advantage in the Cold War. Source 1 also alludes to the technological superiority of America when it states that there was 'no contest' ☞

This is a basic introduction. It does offer several reasons for the end of the Cold War but it would be improved by offering a clear focus on the question, briefly referring to the sources provided, providing an opening judgement and ending with an explicit link to the question.

between the superpowers in this field. Therefore, it is clear that American economic superiority played a highly significant role in ending the Cold War as it meant the USSR could not compete economically and had a vested interest in ending East–West conflict.

Reagan's tough stance on the USSR also contributed to the end of the Cold War. Source 3 points to Reagan introducing a 'moral tone' to the Cold War by calling the USSR an 'evil empire' which put pressure on the Soviet leadership who believed he was 'crazed enough to launch the bomb'. Source 2 also refers to his implementation of the Reagan Doctrine, which put more pressure on the USSR. In 1983 Reagan approved US military intervention in Grenada to remove a left-wing government in Grenada. Such was Reagan's dedication to the doctrine that bore his name, he even supported violent anti-communist regimes, like the Marcos Dictatorship in the Philippines, despite their poor human rights record. Reagan also supplied arms to anti-communist forces in Afghanistan, El Salvador and Nicaragua. This shows Reagan's commitment to stop communist expansionism. Source 3 points to Reagan's policy of pushing the USSR economically through continued commitment to the arms race, making sure there was 'no contest'. This can be seen in 1981 when the Senate approved a 53% increase in the military budget. The commitment to the SDI, and the 7% of the GDP devoted to the military, were clear signs that Reagan was trying to push the USSR into overspend.

Gorbachev also played a key role in the end of the Cold War. Gorbachev's political decisions were a break from Soviet leaders of the past. Source 2 reveals a far less aggressive head of the USSR. He confirmed the Soviet withdrawal of troops from Afghanistan. That Gorbachev was willing to end the Cold War is shown by his involvement in the INF (1987) and START (1991) agreements, which reduced the superpowers' nuclear weapons. Gorbachev was also more open to Western ideas, as shown by his policies of *glasnost* and *perestroika* and his acceptance of political democratisation. Source 2 talks of Gorbachev accepting the 'irresistible forces of democratisation'. He showed his relaxed policy towards Eastern Europe in 1988 when at the 'UN assembly, he cut Warsaw Pact forces by half a million men'. He further showed his commitment to a relaxation of Soviet control over Eastern Europe by abandoning the ☞

This paragraph is much better. It is broadly analytical and shows understanding of the focus of the question. It also develops the argument by cross-referencing Sources 1 and 3 and then integrates the student's own knowledge to add range and depth. In addition, it makes a clear link to the question at the end. Nevertheless, this section has two limitations that would need to be addressed to achieve a higher level: the section on US technological superiority makes no reference at all to Source 3 (which contains relevant material), and the 'economic superiority' argument is not really evaluated.

Here, the student offers another broadly analytical paragraph that again shows some understanding of the focus of the question. The student continues to develop the argument (using Sources 2 and 3) by considering the impact of Reagan's policies. The analysis of the Reagan Doctrine is well supported with own knowledge and explicitly linked to the question at the end. However, the paragraph would be improved by focusing the opening sentence precisely on the question, developing the first statement based on Source 3 with own knowledge and then offering a critical evaluation of the role of Reagan's 'overspend' policies in ending the Cold War.

This paragraph moves on to consider Gorbachev's role in ending the Cold War. On the plus side, the student uses Source 2 and own knowledge quite well to analyse the contribution of the Soviet leader in the late 1980s and early 1990s. However, the paragraph could be improved by making explicit links to the 'economic superiority' argument and putting forward a critical evaluation of the pro-Gorbachev argument in the context of the question.

Brezhnev Doctrine and encouraging democratic reform. This shows that Gorbachev played a significant role in ending the Cold War. He was willing to accept the democratisation of the Soviet Bloc by making it clear 'that the door was now open' (Source 2) so that the satellite states could now walk on 'their own feet' (Source 1).

Popular protest in Eastern Europe was also a key factor in ending the Cold War. Source 2 talks of Gorbachev accepting the 'irresistible forces of democratisation' and this allowed the Soviet satellites to adopt 'Western' economic and political systems. For example, in 1989 Poland elected a non-communist party and in 1990 Hungary adopted a multi-party system. Furthermore in East Germany, Honecker was removed and his replacement, the more liberal Krenz, opened the Berlin Wall in November 1989. This shows that the collapse of communist Eastern Europe was important, as it weakened the Soviet sphere of influence and reversed many communist policies.

In conclusion, despite the importance of the collapse of the Soviet Bloc in Eastern Europe in reducing Soviet power, the role of the Reagan fighting Soviet expansion, and Gorbachev pursuing policies that helped break away from the Cold War, economic factors were most important. It is clear that American economic superiority played the key role in ending the Cold War because it meant that the USSR could not compete economically and had a vested interest in ending East–West hostility.

This penultimate paragraph is quite brief and, like the previous one, lacks a clear focus on the question set. It makes some use of Source 2 and offers the relevant point that the peoples of Eastern Europe opted for 'Western' economic and political reforms. However, once again, there is room for improvement by developing the 'people power' argument and linking it to US economic superiority, connecting the final sentence to the question and offering a critical evaluation of the 'people power' viewpoint.

Although quite short, the conclusion is linked to the question and reaches a judgement about the relative importance of US economic superiority. Nevertheless, this final statement would have been more convincing if the student had developed the case for seeing this factor as the most important.

This is a moderate answer with the qualities of a high level 3 response in AO1 and AO2.

- It shows ability to analyse some key points of the arguments offered in the source material, such as the greater strains imposed on the Soviet economy, Gorbachev's new approach to Cold War diplomacy and Reagan's hard-line stance.
- It reaches a judgement supported by information from the sources and student's own knowledge on 'how far', which relates to US economic superiority.
- It develops some points of support and challenge for the statement in the question by considering US economic superiority, Reagan's 'militarised counter-revolution', Gorbachev's role and 'people power' in Eastern Europe.
- It offers a broadly analytical response from the student's own knowledge, which supports the source material.
- Generally accurate factual material is provided across the 1980s timeframe.
- The argument shows some direction and control but is not sustained; for example, the paragraph on Gorbachev lacks explicit links to the question.
- The answer would be improved by clearly focusing the introduction on the question, by using all the relevant information contained in the sources in the analysis, and by evaluating the strengths and weaknesses of each interpretation.

Overall, this answer achieves **level 3 for both Assessment Objectives and would gain 24 out of 40 marks (10 for AO1a and b, 14 for AO2b).**

**Grade A student answer**

The 1980s saw the beginnings of a permanent thaw in superpower relations, culminating in the renewal of US–Soviet summit diplomacy and the fall of communism in the Eastern Bloc. There is great debate between historians over the factors, which led to this dramatic change, and their relative importance. Some, like Hobsbawm in Source 1, have stressed that America's greater economic strength was a critical factor in ending the Cold War. Other historians, such as Burleigh in Source 3, maintain (in a related way) that it was due to Reagan's pursuit of SDI, which exploited the USA's technological lead over the USSR and forced the Soviets to capitulate. Furthermore, Gaddis in Source 2 identifies two other important causes: Gorbachev's new approach to Cold War relations and the role of 'people power' in Eastern Europe. All four factors contributed to the end of the Cold War, but this essay will conclude that US economic superiority played the most significant part.

As Source 1 points out, America's economic superiority played a key role because even though 'both superpowers overstretched and distorted their economies' due to the hugely expensive arms race, the capitalist system could cope with a $3 trillion US debt. Consequently, Reagan was able to pressure the USSR by increasing military spending by 53% in the 1980s (designed in part to develop the B1 bomber, neutron bomb and stealth aircraft programmes, expand the US navy, and deploy MX missiles). In contrast, as both Source 1 and Source 2 acknowledge, economic pressures were working to 'degrade the Soviet system' (Source 2). To keep up with the USA (whose military costs amounted to 7 per cent of GDP), the USSR was spending about 25% of its GDP on the military at a time when Soviet industrial growth was falling from 2 to 0% between 1980 and 1987. The larger and more efficient US economy was clearly at an advantage. On becoming leader, Gorbachev realised this was an unsustainable situation: the arms race had to end to release funds to improve economic and social conditions in the USSR.

The USA held another major economic advantage because the USSR incurred heavy costs in maintaining the satellite states and their socialist allies. These countries acted as a 'constant and vast annual drain' (Source 1) on the Soviet economy, partly because of the need to 'maintain control over unwilling peoples' (Source 2). The Warsaw Pact members, for example, ☞

This is a good, straightforward introduction that focuses on the question, outlines the competing arguments by briefly referring to all the sources provided and offers a clear opening judgement to make the intended line of argument immediately apparent.

This is a focused paragraph. Sources 1 and 2 are cross-referenced confidently to develop the 'US economic superiority' argument. Short quotations from these extracts are used effectively to help build the case. The student has also integrated appropriate own knowledge to add range and depth to the source-based analysis. At the end, however, the link to the question is implicit rather than explicit. This is a shame because the rest of the paragraph offers good analysis.

received a yearly oil subsidy of some $3 billion from the Soviet Union and Cuba was given $4 billion in aid and subsidies between 1981 and 1986. America's economic superiority was also demonstrated in the field of technology. According to Source 1 and Source 3, there was 'no contest' in this area because the USSR could not compete with the USA 'in the most advanced computer and laser technologies'. From this perspective, Reagan's announcement of the SDI in 1983 put further economic pressure on the USSR to keep up and exposed the Soviets' outdated technology. Ultimately, US economic superiority (in terms of financial strength and advanced technology) persuaded the USSR to abandon the Cold War before the Soviet economy reached breaking point.

Gaddis, in Source 2, challenges the 'economic superiority' view by emphasising the major role played by Gorbachev in ending the Cold War. His radically new approach to East–West relations abandoned old style Soviet attitudes so that the Reagan Doctrine 'was pushing at an open door'. Gorbachev transformed the international situation by cutting the Soviet 'ground force commitment to the Warsaw Pact', abandoning the Brezhnev Doctrine, and entering into productive arms negotiations with Reagan and Bush. The latter culminated in the INF Treaty (1987), which removed a whole class of intermediate nuclear weapons, and the 1991 START Agreement, which reduced overall nuclear arsenals by 30%. Nevertheless, even allowing for Gorbachev's obvious personal impact, the Soviet leader's Cold War policies were to a large extent driven by an inability to compete with US superiority and the need to address the USSR's mounting economic and social problems. Furthermore, it was Reagan's 'horror of nuclear weapons' (Source 3) and his willingness to set aside his deeply held anti-communism, which made the US relationship with Gorbachev productive.

'People power' in Eastern Europe, as Gaddis briefly notes in Source 2, also played a role in bringing the Cold War to a close. Taking their cue from Gorbachev (who had renounced the Brezhnev Doctrine and advocated 'freedom of choice' in 1988), the peoples of Eastern Europe – 'the irresistible forces of democratisation' – removed the satellite regimes quickly and in a largely peaceful manner. However, popular pressure in the former Soviet Bloc pushed the process much further than the loose federation of 'liberalised' socialist states Gorbachev hoped for. The failures of central ☞

This paragraph is also focused on the question. It develops the argument by considering the economic burden the Soviet Empire placed on the USSR and the USA's technological superiority. Like the last paragraph, the sources are cross-referenced confidently to establish the case and relevant student knowledge is integrated to reinforce the points taken from the extracts. An examiner would be pleased to see that the student has used statistics to support the argument. There is also a clear link to the question at the end. The paragraph could be improved though, at the end, with an evaluation of the strengths and weaknesses of the 'economic superiority' viewpoint.

In examining Gorbachev's role, this paragraph challenges the 'economic superiority' argument. The student builds on relevant information taken from Source 2 by using appropriate own knowledge to develop the pro-Gorbachev interpretation. This time, however, the paragraph is stronger. It is rounded off with a critical evaluation of Gorbachev's contribution, which not only acknowledges Reagan's role but also links back clearly to the question.

economic planning, and growing trade links with the West during the 1970s, made East Europeans aware of higher Western living standards. Consequently, in 1989, they dismantled the Soviet Bloc and opted for the 'superior' Western-style economic (and political) systems. In this sense too, US (and Western) economic superiority undermined the legitimacy of the Soviet Bloc and helped to end the Cold War.

Overall, US economic superiority was the key factor, which ended the Cold War because, as Source 1 argues, 'there was nobody to take the equivalent strain on Soviet expenditure'. Moreover, American economic strength underpinned other influential factors. Reagan's 'militarised counter-revolution', which was designed to squeeze the Soviet economy into submission, relied on superior American resources. Furthermore, Gorbachev's New Political Thinking was based on the need to reform the Soviet economy and the recognition that the USSR could not compete with the USA in a renewed arms race. Finally, Eastern Europe's demand for change stemmed partly from the popular conviction that a capitalist system would lead to higher living standards.

> Another focused and developed paragraph that uses the brief reference to Eastern Europe in Source 2 to good effect. The student's own knowledge is deployed thoughtfully here to link 'people power' in the Soviet Bloc to popular demands for 'Western' economic and political reforms. Furthermore, the paragraph ends with an explicit link to the question.

> The conclusion is clearly linked to the main analysis and shows how US economic superiority influenced the other factors discussed in the essay. It is focused on the question and reaches an overall judgement on the 'economic superiority' argument.

This is a good answer.

- It interprets the sources with confidence as revealed, for example, by the paragraph on the cost of the Soviet empire and technology.
- It shows understanding of the arguments in the extracts and relates them to wider knowledge of the issues throughout.
- Discussion of the issues is based on source analysis and student's own knowledge in every main paragraph.
- It reaches and sustains a conclusion that makes a clear judgement about the importance of US economic superiority.
- The student's own knowledge supports and is integrated with the analysis of the presented source material; this can be seen, for instance, in the paragraph on increased US military spending.
- The student's own knowledge is accurate, relevant and demonstrates range and depth across the 1980s timeframe.
- The answer would be improved by ensuring that all links to the question in the essay are explicit and that the strengths and weaknesses of each interpretation are evaluated.

Overall, this answer achieves **level 4 for both Assessment Objectives and would gain 32 out of 40 marks (13 for AO1a and b, 19 for AO2b).**

# Index